INTERPRETING
DReams A-Z

LIFE Styles

Hay House, Inc.
Carlsbad, California
Sydney, Australia

Leon Nacson

Published and distributed in the United States by:

Hay House, Inc., P.O. Box 5100, Carlsbad, CA 92018-5100 • (800) 654-5126 • (800) 650-5115 (fax)

Editorial supervision: Jill Kramer   Design: Jenny Richards   Author's researcher/editor: Rachel Eldred

The author of this book does not dispense medical advice or prescribe the use of any technique as a form of treatment for physical or medical problems without the advice of a physician, either directly or indirectly. The intent of the author is only to offer information of a general nature to help you in your quest for emotional and spiritual well-being. In the event you use any of the information in this book for yourself, which is your constitutional right, the author and the publisher assume no responsibility for your actions.

Library of Congress Cataloging-in-Publication Data

Nacson, Leon.
        Interpreting dreams A–Z / Leon Nacson.
           p.   cm.
        ISBN 1-56170-576-4 (hardcover) • 1-56170-789-9 (tradepaper)
           1. Dream interpretation—Dictionaries.   2. Dreams—Dictionaries.
        3. Symbolism (Psychology)—Dictionaries.   I.   Title.
        BF1091.N16   1999
        154.6'3—dc21   98-37483
                                                                                      CIP

ISBN 1-56170-576-4

04 03 02 01   5 4 3 2

1st printing, July 1999

2nd printing, August 2001

Printed in China through Palace Press International

DEDICATION
To Leon, Stella, Angelo, Mary, and Umberto. My dearest Nona and Nono.

Contents

Foreword

by Deepak Chopra, M.D.

"O sleep, O gentle sleep. Nature's soft nurse." — William Shakespeare

I have always been fascinated with dreams, and have enjoyed the many conversations Leon and I have had on the subject. We agree that without a good night's sleep, our dream state cannot be fully utilized. With this in mind, I thought it would be useful to introduce this book with my thoughts on how to enjoy a blissful night's rest.

In the USA, one out of every three adults experiences periodic trouble sleeping, and each year at least 10,000 Americans consult a physician about their sleep. It's a concern that often promotes anxiety. Understandably so. Wanting to sleep but being unable to *is* frustrating. The good news is that there are many ways to promote and encourage a good night's sleep.

You can't command sleep. The harder you try, the less successful you will be and the more frustrated you will become. Instead, the best attitude to adopt is an attitude I call "not minding." In other words, don't become a commentator on your own dilemma. Rather, rest comfortably, "not minding." Lie in bed with your eyes closed, not caring if you are awake or asleep.

The mere act of remaining motionless with your eyes closed (even if you are feeling anxious or restless) provides your body with significant benefits. Be aware of how uncomfortable you may be feeling. If you are feeling discomfort in your body, bring your awareness to that discomfort. Allow your awareness to acknowledge the sensations, and even if you are feeling restless, uncomfortable, or fidgety, recognize that these feelings represent the process of healing taking place.

Getting in touch with yourself is important if you want to enjoy a restful night's sleep, and knowledge of Ayurveda helps us understand *how* our body functions.

Ayurveda is India's ancient system of medicine, and it has been employed for over 5,000 years. Meaning "science of life" in Sanskrit,

Ayurveda teaches that there are three basic body types (doshas). These three basic Ayurvedic doshas are Vata, Pitta, and Kapha. Each of us needs all three doshas to build and sustain a healthy body, although most of us will find that one or two doshas tend to dominate.

Those with a dominant Vata dosha tend to have light or restless sleep. Those with a dominant Pitta usually sleep soundly. If sleeping problems do arise, they usually involve waking up in the middle of the night and feeling overheated. Kapha types sleep deeply and soundly, and, if anything, have a tendency to oversleep.

The Vata, Pitta, and Kapha doshas also dominate certain parts of the day. From six to ten A.M. or P.M., an influence of Kapha is dominant in the environment; from ten to two A.M. or P.M., an influence of Pitta is more dominant; and from two to six A.M. or P.M., Vata dominates.

If you attune your daily routine to this 24-hour cycle, you'll find restful sleep more attainable. According to Ayurveda, the best time to go to bed is no later than ten P.M. This is when the Kapha period dominates, and it's

Kapha that tends to promote deep, sound sleep. In other words, the influence on the environment is supportive of sleep. Conversely, Ayurveda ideally recommends getting up at six A.M., and no later than seven A.M., because this is when Vata dominates; and Vata favors alertness, lightness, activity, and quickness of mental and physical functions.

There's no need to force this routine upon yourself. It can be achieved slowly. Simply begin by waking a few minutes earlier each morning and going to bed a few minutes earlier each night. Over a period of a week, you'll find yourself arising 15 to 30 minutes earlier every morning. Use an alarm clock to help you adjust until that time when you can wake up naturally.

If modern-day excitement entices you to ignore Ayurvedic rhythm, then preparing for sleep may at first seem like a thoroughly foreign activity. Following are five recommendations to help promote a restful night's sleep:

1. Eat a light dinner early, ideally between 5:30 and 7 P.M. A heavy or late supper will take a longer time to digest. Digestion involves increased metabolic activity that works against a settled and relaxed sleep.

2. Take a short 5- or 15-minute stroll after dinner to promote relaxation and aid digestion.

3. Avoid exciting, dynamic, or focused activity in the evening. Many people find that they get wound up during the evening and then have difficulty unwinding and falling asleep. If you must attend to some focused activity, or do have to work at night, stop by nine P.M. at the latest.

4. Avoid watching television in the evening. I know this might sound like a tall order for many people, but for anyone who sleeps restlessly, it's very helpful. Television, even programs that seem relaxing, is actually inherently exciting to the nervous system. It stimulates, and even overstimulates, sight, hearing, and overall mental functioning.

5. If you like to read before going to bed, do your reading in a room other than the bedroom. The bedroom should be associated with sleeping, not with mental activity such as reading or watching television.

A good night's sleep is one of the best gifts you can give yourself. After a sound sleep, you wake up feeling recharged and vibrant; you have a sense of vitality that lasts throughout the day. A restful night's sleep also gives you greater access to your dreams, which, in turn, can bring you to a deeper understanding of yourself.

Sweet dreams!

Interpreting Your Dreams—
What You Need to Know

Human beings have always been intrigued by their dreams. In ancient Rome, dreams were regarded as prophetic, and decisions were often influenced by them. In the second century A.D., a Greek physician named Artemidorus wrote a dream interpretation book called *Oneirocritica*.

Travel two millennia further back in time to ancient Egypt, and we find evidence of recorded dreams in hieroglyphs. Then, of course, there are the great dream cultures such as the American Indians, Australian Aborigines, and Malaysian Senoi, each of which has a very intimate and unique relationship to the dream world.

If we turn our attention to modern history, we find a plethora of literature available on dreams. In the West, many have yearned to find out more about humanity through dream interpretation, most notably Sigmund Freud and Carl Jung. Today, there are hundreds of books available on the subject.

Given all the information available, trying to decipher the meaning of your dreams can be confusing. But dreams are our private universe—and you are the ultimate interpreter of this universe. Only you, as the one who experiences your dreams, can interpret them correctly. However, there are pointers that can help you decipher the meaning of your dreams. Given this basic premise, I present to you a coach's manual on dream interpretation, rather than a definitive guide.

Just as cookbooks, auto repair guides, and instruction manuals of all sorts provide guidance on how to cook up a feast, fix your car, or program a video, this book, too, will coach you—and encourage you—to become your own expert dream interpreter. Within these pages, you will find an A–Z guide to dream symbology. It's important to remember that none of the definitions are absolute—they can't be.

Throughout history, humans have redefined and reinterpreted the world around them.

We once thought that the earth was flat and that storks delivered babies! Cigarette smoking is a poignant example of how our world can be redefined. In the 1950s, smoking was advertised as therapeutic; doctors would recommend it as a means of stress relief. Today, of course, we know that the opposite is true. Most of us are aware of how unhealthful cigarette smoking can be—and we are now cognizant of the dangers associated with passive smoking, too. During the 1950s, dreaming about smoking might have given rise to a different interpretation than it would today. Dreams reflect both archetypal images and the changing, fluid meanings that we ascribe to our world.

An interesting finding I came across recently concerned dreaming in space. NASA did a study on astronauts and found that in their dreams, everything floats, imitating the conditions of weightlessness in space. In a dream about picking a flower, they would float over to the flower, which would also be floating. This shows that dream states often match the immediate condition of our environment.

Because dreams can relate specifically to your environment and situation, after each dream symbol entry, I have left enough space for you—the ultimate dream interpreter—to add your own personal interpretation of the symbol. My interpretations are to be used as prompters, encouraging you to think about these symbols.

Although symbols are fluid, there are—and always have been—universal meanings among humans. Hand and facial gestures can help us communicate with people all over the world; and symbols, too, help us bridge the language barrier. People everywhere identify with symbols such as the Christian cross, the Star of David, the yin/yang symbol, the astrological signs—or McDonald's golden arches! True, each person has their own individual understanding of these symbols, yet a universal meaning also exists. The golden arches have grown to symbolize fast food, whether or not you want to sink your teeth into a Big Mac.

We all dream—that is a fact! Some will say they never dream—but sleep studies have proven that everyone dreams, whether or not they remember them. Each night we experience another dimension where people, places, and objects from our waking reality ignore the constraints of time and space, and play out new scenarios in our mind's eye. Some people remember their dreams easily; others don't. For those

with good recall, dreamtime can be an exciting, weird, and wonderful part of life.

In our dreams, we can do the seemingly impossible, switching identities, places, and situations in a matter of milliseconds. Our dream world is a wonderful place of invention and imagination. Yet it is a lot more than this. Plato, Aristotle, Descartes, Freud, and Jung all postulated that dreams are windows to understanding the human mind, and, indeed, represent aspects of an individual's life.

Dreams can tell you about yourself and bring you face-to-face with your hidden talents and potential. Scientific evidence suggests that dreams can indicate our emotional and psychological states in the same way that a urine test can clue us in on our physical state. Our dreamtime experiences can provide us with important information that helps us grow and evolve. The key is for *you* to interpret your dreams, using this information on dream interpretation only as a guide.

We all have a unique connection to our dreams, and just as physical exercise produces results, so too will our work on intuition assist us in understanding our dream messages. The important thing is to relax and have fun with dream interpretation. It's not to be taken too seriously or to be imbued with grave prophetic significance. Treat dream interpretation as an adventure, and you will enjoy your journey to greater self-understanding.

Starting on page xvii, I have provided a short reference guide on Dream Language, which lists the most common words and phrases used in dream interpretation, along with their definitions. But first, a brief introduction to methods of interpreting your dreams.

Methods of Dream Interpretation

There are many methods of dream interpretation. How you choose to interpret your dreams is less important than the personal meaning they hold for you. Yet, the following suggestions will certainly assist you in exploring your dream world. Choose what works best for you.

(Please remember that dreams can either be looked at individually or studied collectively over a period of time. For example, you may want to look over a number of dreams during a particularly stressful period of your life to gather input and assistance.)

1. Create your own dream dictionary. Buy a lined notebook, and record the symbols you remember from your dreams. Beside each word, enter your meaning for that symbol.

For example, you may enter *apple*, then beside it, write *health*, *teacher*, *forbidden fruit*. Over time, you will build up your own personal dream dictionary. (You might also want to use my *Dream Journal*, also published by Hay House.)

2. Notice the feelings that come up during your dreams. Just as you can be tired or invigorated after a hard day's work, so too can you be tired or invigorated after a heavy night's dreaming. When you wake up, reflect on your feelings and emotions. They can help you understand the symbols you remember from your dream.

3. Talk with someone you consider to be wise. Talk about different viewpoints on life—but listen more than you talk. General conversation and sharing of feelings can provide you with valuable information for dream interpretation.

4. Draw your dream or make a collage. Doing this can help you understand a vivid, emotional, or thought-provoking dream. Keep the project personal while you're creating it. Let your intuition govern the project, unaffected by outside influences.

5. Become the symbol. This technique from psychologist Fritz Perls is one of the most useful in dream interpretation. If you dreamed that you were walking down a tunnel, bring that experience to your daytime reality. Close your eyes and say, "I am walking down a tunnel now." Then, in your mind, slowly *become* the tunnel. When you remember a dream, you refer to it in the past tense and think about it with a conscious mind. When you say, "I am walking

down a tunnel," you are in the present tense, which allows you to access the same alpha patterns you had in the dream. By becoming the symbol, you detach from the situation and gain a different perspective.

6. Read books and listen to tapes and seminars available on the subject. Search magazines and papers for articles on the mind, thinking, and dreaming. Don't forget your family. Start with the oldest members. They can often give you insight into your ancestors. Also, go to the movies and watch videos, keeping an eye out for any pertinent information that provokes an "ah-ha" reaction.

7. Avoid sleeping pills—they alter the dream process. If you do have trouble falling asleep, look for natural alternatives rather than pharmaceutical drugs. (See the foreword for some helpful tips from Deepak Chopra.)

Finally, when you wake up from a dream, consider what it means to you, and consult your dream dictionary about the message it contains. If you are interpreting for other people, assist them, but don't judge. Simply guide them, and let them interpret their own dreams.

About Your Dream Dictionary

I believe that creating your own dream dictionary is the most essential aspect of dream interpretation. Therefore, to assist you in creating a dream dictionary, I've provided a quick overview on some of the major dream subjects. The following will help you understand the individual symbols in your dreams.

Animals

What does the animal represent to you? Do you feel it is supportive, or is it threatening? It's important to look at your cultural background for any significance. Different cultures have their own individual association with different animals. For example, the owl can be seen as a symbol of wisdom or desolation, as sacred or evil, or as a predator or a symbol of crime.

The Body

We often relate our feelings to the body. We say that "it touches my heart," or "he's a pain in the neck." One way to work with these images is to first ask yourself, *Is it my body? Someone else's? Is it part of an animal?* Next, ask, *How am I (or are they) affected by that part of the body? Then ask, How does the situation in the dream affect them/me?*

Death

Dying in a dream rarely means that someone is going to die. It usually means transformation, change, or renewal. It may be a mental funeral for your current problem.

Feelings

There are four fundamental feelings associated with dreams: fear, frustration, joy, and detachment.

1. *Fear* may be telling you that you are unable to cope with a certain confrontation in life.

2. *Frustration* usually signifies a lack of fulfillment, as well as dissatisfaction.

3. *Joy* indicates contentment, and suggests that happiness will follow.

4. *Detachment* is observing a situation without attaching emotion to it; you are unconcerned about the outcome.

Food

Food is essential for energy. When you see it in a dream, the feeling around the food is very important. Does it fulfill you? Is it easy to chew? Is it healthy or fattening? Does it represent joy or pain? Where does the food come from? Is it tropical and full of life, or is it a staple food? Who gave you the food? Do you feel there is enough food to sustain you or not enough? Carefully look at what the food represents to you to fully comprehend its symbology in a dream.

Geographical Locations

Dreaming of another country may indicate an unconscious craving. First, write down what that country means to you and how it is currently perceived. Second, compare how it was perceived in its golden age to how it is perceived now.

Dreaming of foreign shores can spark past-life memories. In the dream state, many people have had vivid past-life experiences that involve another country. Traveling to these places for the first time, they realize that their dream was accurate.

Again, dreaming of foreign lands will have different connotations for a travel agent than it will for someone about to embark on a journey. Or, it may be that the pizza you had for dinner reminds you of Italy!

Home

In a dream, your home is generally thought to relate to your body, and each story has a different meaning. For example, the basement refers to the subliminal aspects of the psyche—our innate sexuality and other aspects of the unconscious. Ground level is our current reality; it deals with what is happening in our conscious, every-day lives. The upper level deals with the intellect and your outlook on life—you're looking at things from a higher perspective to see the overall picture. The roof refers to spiritual aspirations.

Journeys

When you dream of traveling, the nature of the journey is as important as the vehicle used to take the trip. Why did you get on the plane or bike? How secure did you feel? How did you feel when you arrived at your destination? Did you arrive? Today, the automobile, like the house, can represent the self as long as it is your own vehicle.

Money

When you dream about money—whether you receive it or give it away—see it as a form of valuable energy. It's okay to feel good about money and abundance in a dream.

If you remove the guilt associated with abundance, you can move toward understanding the true nature of this energy. The more abundance, the more choices.

Music

View music in a dream in light of your own experience. A musician may view it as abundance. If you're not a musician, you may be tapping into a hidden desire to be creative. Focus on the tune and the person playing the instrument rather than on the instrument.

People

Pay particular attention to the people in your dreams. Are they the same as in real life? How do you feel about them? Are they related to you? Are they business associates? How do you feel about their age, occupation, state of well-being, or lifestyle? Do you like them? Do you feel the same way about them in the dream as you do in life? What about strangers—did they attract or repulse you?

Places of Worship

Fritz Perls's technique is useful here—simply *become* the place of worship. Consider how you feel about the structure and its surroundings.

Seasons

Spring indicates new ideas, perhaps an awakening. Summer tells of harvest, light and heat, holidays, and an abundant supply of nature's fruits. Autumn implies that things are coming to an end, and winter indicates hibernation—a time of inner development but little outward progress.

Just as a swimming coach shows people how to swim in water, the suggestions presented in this book are designed to help you "swim" when it comes to dream interpretation. The idea is for you to become the best—and most expert—interpreter of your dreams. It's a journey that encourages greater insight and understanding into who you are, and that also gives you a glimpse into what you are capable of becoming.

It's fun, too!

DREAM LANGUAGE

Here is a list of the words and concepts used most often in discussions and literature about dreams. Read them and make yourself familiar with them. On a separate piece of paper, feel free to add any other terms you've found helpful on your dream journey.

alpha rhythm
Refers to brainwave activity. Alpha rhythm is the half-asleep/half-awake state, a state of deep relaxation, or the state we are in before we drift off to sleep.

archetype
Carl Jung used the term to describe the essential nature of human existence in its various representations as it is passed down from generation to generation according to race. For example, there is the archetype of the wise old man or woman, or the hero/heroine.

association
A subjective process of linking concepts or ideas by allowing one concept to suggest another in a spontaneous fashion.

astral plane
The dimension experienced when one feels "free" from the constraints of the human body.

astral traveling
The phenomenon of *experiencing* our spirit/soul "outside" the physical body. A feeling of being free from the constraints of the human body.

beta rhythm
This brainwave rhythm refers to the active, assessing, decision-making brain; the daily "awake" state of being.

consciousness
The state of being aware of our acts, activities, and reactions.

delta rhythm
This is the slowest brain rhythm. It occurs when we are so fast asleep that we are unconscious, or when we are anesthetized. A fetus in the womb also registers this brainwave.

dialoguing
Conversing with ourselves about our feelings, thoughts, and actions. This includes having an imaginary chat (when we are awake) with people who are featured in our dreams.

dream coach
With the right guidance, advice, and knowledge, a dream coach assists an individual in finding individual answers to their dreams.

dream lover
Someone you have a romantic or erotic encounter with in a dream.

dream motif
A recurring theme, action, or situation in a dream state.

dream reentry
Reentering a dream while you are awake to reexperience it and perhaps bring it to completion. Helpful for nightmares and recurring dreams.

electroencephalograph/EEG
A device used to measure brainwaves.

hypnagogic sleep
Refers to the images we may see as we drift off to sleep. They have been referred to as "dreamlets," although they are not dreams because they are not accompanied by rapid eye movement (REM).

hypnopompic hallucinations
Occur when the brain is still in a dream state even though the eyes are open. The dreamer may confuse external objects with their dream images. The images may even be superimposed on the waking scene.

insomnium dreams

Artemidorus, a Greek physician who lived in the second century A.D., referred to insomnium dreams as those that reflected the dreamer's current physical and mental state.

latent dreams

A term used by Sigmund Freud to describe dreams that were clear and precise—that is, unadulterated.

lucid dreaming

Being aware that you're dreaming when you're in a dream state.

mandala

The sacred circle representing wholeness and unity. Clustering your dream symbols within a mandala (circle) will encourage integration and wholeness.

manifest dreams

Sigmund Freud used this term to mean those dreams that were censored—that is, bizarre and confusing.

nightmare

A dream that incites anxiety, and in which fearful events occur and/or fearful images/symbols appear. In medieval Europe, the word was used to refer to an attack by the night demon; the "mare" was a demon. Research has recorded a phenomenon that gives credence to the concept of a "mare"; people have reported waking up paralyzed and seeing some kind of entity in their room. Today, this phenomenon is called a "paralysis attack."

precognitive dreams

Dreams that provide the dreamer with answers to everyday concerns. They can predict future events and give insightful information on how to solve a problem. They may also validate the direction we are taking in life.

prodomic dreams

Dreams that warn us of any existing or future health problems.

rapid eye movement (REM)

REM occurs while we're asleep, and refers to the rapid movement of our eyes. We dream during REM sleep.

recurring dreams

Dreams that recur within a given period. They often address an important issue we are not facing in our waking life. Recurring dreams are not necessarily carbon-copy dreams; they may simply involve recurring themes.

serial dreams

A series of dreams in which there seems to be some logical progression—same people, same places, same theme—and each is obviously a continuation from the last dream scene.

sleep paralysis

Refers to the inability to move our muscles during the dream state. The only muscles active in sleep are the eyes and the chest muscles. A part of the brain (pons) turns the rest of the muscles off. Research has shown this to be a safety mechanism to stop us from harming ourselves while we're dreaming.

sleeptalking and sleepwalking

Walking or talking while asleep. Contrary to popular belief, these phenomena do not occur during stage one of sleep—that is, the dream state. They are not an "acting-out" of the dream. (See "sleep paralysis.")

somnium dreams

These dreams, defined by the ancient Greek physician, Artemidorus, were prophetic and highly symbolic. Artemidorus created a dream interpretation dictionary for them.

subconscious

Describes that which we are not immediately aware of but which can be brought to consciousness. Sigmund Freud described it as the transition zone in which repressed material must pass from the unconscious to the conscious. Also, that in which we are faintly aware.

synchronicity

Refers to any situation in which our inner and outer environments coincide to produce meaning—for example, if you are thinking about certain friends and they call or drop by.

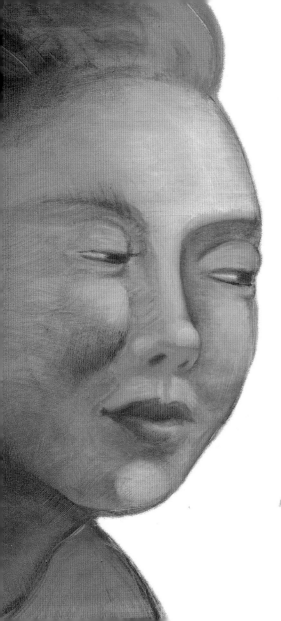

theta rhythm
The brainwave rhythm experienced while we sleep and dream.

unconscious
That of which we have no awareness. In psychoanalysis, it is the region of the mind that houses repression and the id.

The dream on the next page is used as an example of how this dream dictionary can work for you.

Sample Dream

*I am walking through a park when suddenly an airplane appears.
I board the plane, and it takes off. Inside the plane are people I went
to school with. I am covered in spiders. I wake up.*

The first thing to do is write down the symbols. In this case, they would be: **airplane, school friends, spiders.** You then refer to what has been written under the appropriate symbol in this book—for example, **airplane.**

Airplane

Possible Meanings: Defying gravity (that is, laws of nature); rapid movement; freedom; uninhibited thoughts; travel.

Points to Consider: Are you frightened of traveling? Are you in control of the airplane? Are you being taken for a ride?

Your Interpretation:

The *Possible Meanings* help you determine the nature of your dream, and the *Points to Consider* act as prompters so you can delve more fully into your dream. In *Your Interpretation*, add your own comments and thoughts.

In my dream above, the airplane represents transportation. I am being transported back to the past. One of the meanings given for spiders is being misunderstood. Therefore, a simple explanation of my dream would be traveling back in time to a place where I am misunderstood.

Each dream symbol not only presents you with an indication of what the symbol may mean, but also takes you one step further and encourages you to uncover your own meaning. As a coach, I offer guidance into dream interpretation so you can unlock the secrets of your dream world while having a great time, too.

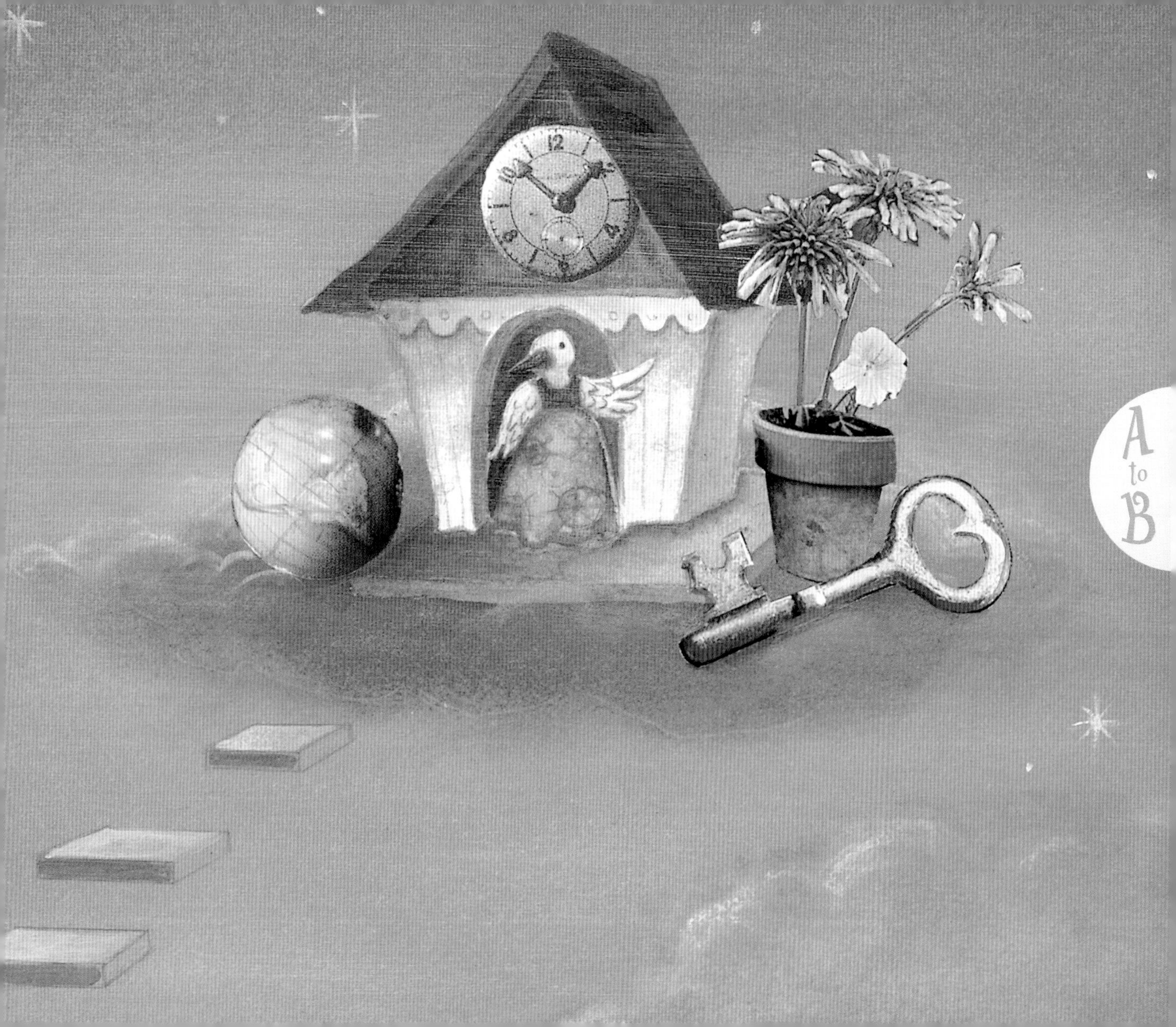
A to B

A
to
B

The A-Z List of Dream Symbols

Actor

Possible Meanings: Pretense, disguise, illusion, ulterior motives, stardom.

Points to Consider: Who is the actor in your dream? Are you acting? Is the actor taking part in a comedy, drama, mystery, thriller, etc?

Your Interpretation:

Angel

Possible Meanings: Protection, support, messenger, guidance, divine intervention.

Points to Consider: Do you need guidance? Are you looking for a sign? Is the angel imparting a message to you?

Your Interpretation:

Airplane

Possible Meanings: Defying gravity (that is, laws of nature); rapid movement; freedom; uninhibited thoughts; travel.

Points to Consider: Are you frightened of traveling? Are you in control of the airplane? Are you being taken for a ride?

Your Interpretation:

Animals

See "Animals," page xiii.

Antiques

Possible Meanings: Value, the past, preservation, workmanship, rarity.

Points to Consider: Are you surrounded by outdated ideas? Are your old ideas still valued today? How are you unique from others?

Your Interpretation:

Applause

Possible Meanings: Respect, adulation, acceptance, noisy presence, clearing of energy.

Points to Consider: Do you crave acknowledgment? Have you trivialized something? Are you being shown the respect you deserve?

Your Interpretation:

Ants

Possible Meanings: Organization, hard work, structure, devotion to duty, inner strength.

Points to Consider: Are you being asked to perform supernatural tasks? Is your life too orderly? Are you working too hard?

Your Interpretation:

Apple

Possible Meanings: Acknowledgment (giving teacher an apple), forbidden fruit, computers (Apple Macintosh), health, abundance.

Points to Consider: Are you concerned about your health? Do you need a computer? Do you need to acknowledge someone?

Your Interpretation:

Arm

See "Body Parts," page 13; and "The Body," page xiii.

Arrow

Possible Meanings: Flight, getting straight to the point, message, battle, infliction of pain.

Points to Consider: Should you be more direct in life? Is it time to be more self-motivated? Do you or does someone else in your life need to get straight to the point?

Your Interpretation:

Attic

Possible Meanings: Lofty thoughts, higher consciousness, elevated communication, storage, sanctuary.

Points to Consider: What in your life do you want to bring to higher ground? Is it time to put ideas into action? Are you being overwhelmed by your thoughts?

Your Interpretation:

Automobile

See "Car," page 24.

Baby

Possible Meanings: New beginnings, commitments, bundle of joy, expansion of ideas, growth.

Points to Consider: Are you the baby? Whose baby is it? Is the baby self-sufficient?

Your Interpretation:

Bakery

Possible Meanings: Sustenance, making money (dough), bringing an idea to completion, earning a living, early starts.

Points to Consider: What is being transformed? Is it time for change? Are you looking for warmth and support?

Your Interpretation:

Back

See "Body Parts," page 13; and "The Body," page xiii.

Ball (dance)

Possible Meanings: Gathering, in harmony with others, looking your best, formality, invitations.

Points to Consider: Were you invited to a ball? Are you an observer? Do you wish to be in harmony with others?

Your Interpretation:

Balloon

Possible Meanings: Inflation, expansion, reshaping, flexibility, joy.

Points to Consider: Do you feel there is a need for expansion in your life? Are you full of hot air? Are you floating along in life?

Your Interpretation:

....

....

....

....

Bank

Possible Meanings: Safety, protection, red tape, abundance, lack.

Points to Consider: Can others bank on you? Are you in a bank? Are you depositing or withdrawing money?

Your Interpretation:

....

....

....

....

Bar

Possible Meanings: Sociability, intoxication, escape, relaxation, work.

Points to Consider: Are you in the bar? Are you looking into a bar? Are you working in a bar?

Your Interpretation:

Barn

Possible Meanings: Storage, love of animals, exile, shelter, stability.

Points to Consider: Are you in the barn? Is someone else in the barn? Are you focused on creating or creation (Jesus was born in a barn)?

Your Interpretation:

Baseball

Possible Meanings: Big catch, hitting hard, covering bases, home runs, curve balls.

Points to Consider: Are you playing or watching? Are you being counted on by your team players? Are all bases covered?

Your Interpretation:

Basement

Possible Meanings: The subconscious, hidden thoughts, storage, dampness, foundation.

Points to Consider: Are you in the basement, or is someone else in the basement? Are you burying something? Is it time to remove something from your life?

Your Interpretation:

Bath

Possible Meanings: Immersion, healing, cleansing, renewal, possible financial setbacks (took a bath in the market).

Points to Consider: Are you or is someone else taking a bath? Is there a commercial aspect to consider regarding this dream? Is your association with the bath pleasurable or therapeutic?

Your Interpretation:

Bats

Possible Meanings: Seeing in the dark, sensing, heightened intuition, looking at things differently, mistaken identity.

Points to Consider: Are your thoughts on the right track (or am I looking at the world upside down)? Are you flying blind? Is your life's blood (spirit) being sucked out?

Your Interpretation:

....

....

....

....

Beach

Possible Meanings: Relaxation, underlying currents, change, union, observation, being seen.

Points to Consider: Are you on the beach, or are you watching people on the beach? Do you feel safe or in danger? What size are the waves, and what is causing them (currents, winds, pressure)?

Your Interpretation:

....

....

....

....

Bear

See "Animals," page xiii.

Bed

Possible Meanings: Rest, sexual encounters, misadventures (you've made your bed—now lie in it), sanctuary, tossing and turning.

Points to Consider: Who is in the bed? Are you alone, or are you taking someone to bed? Do you want to get out of bed?

Your Interpretation:

....

....

....

....

interpreting dreams a-z

Beer

Possible Meanings: Fermentation, big head, celebration, thirst quencher, sociability.

Points to Consider: Are you drinking the beer? Are you offering the beer to someone else? Is there someone in your life who is all show (big head)?

Your Interpretation:

Bees

Possible Meanings: Industriousness, loyalty, servitude, sweetness, stinging.

Points to Consider: Are you on a natural high at the moment (buzzing)? Are you cross-pollinating ideas? Who is the honey (sweetness) for?

Your Interpretation:

Bells

Possible Meanings: Announcements, commitment, clearing of energy, noise, high ideals.

Points to Consider: What/who is trying to get your attention? Is there an announcement you would like to make? Is something/someone asking for greater commitment?

Your Interpretation:

Bicycle

Possible Meanings: Movement, transportation, balance, exercise.

Points to Consider: Are you riding the bike, or are you watching someone else ride the bike? Do you want to maintain balance in your life? Do you feel you may fall over if you stop moving?

Your Interpretation:

Bird

Possible Meanings: Messages, freedom, overview, moving ahead (early bird gets the worm), vision.

Points to Consider: Are you (or the bird) free or in a cage? Do you want to move to a higher perch? Are you carrying an important message?

Your Interpretation:

....

....

....

....

Birth

Possible Meanings: Completion, new beginnings, a release, duplication of self, new arrival.

Points to Consider: Are you giving birth to new ideas or relationships? Is someone else giving birth? Have you felt a huge release/relief in your life recently—or is there one on the horizon?

Your Interpretation:

....

....

....

....

Blackboard

Possible Meanings: Ideas, punishment, transition, irritation (fingernails down the blackboard), knowledge.

Points to Consider: Are you writing on the blackboard? Are you reading from a blackboard? Are you acquiring knowledge or being punished?

Your Interpretation:

....

....

....

....

Blanket

Possible Meanings: Security, warmth, superficial covering, lack of vision (blanket of fog), comfort.

Points to Consider: Are you on top of or under the blanket? Are you fully covered or exposed? Is it keeping you warm, or are you misusing it?

Your Interpretation:

....

....

....

....

Blindness

Possible Meanings: No vision, other senses heightened, in the dark, need guidance, confidence.

Points to Consider: What are you blind to? What other senses do you prefer be heightened? What do you need to do to see things differently?

Your Interpretation:

....

....

....

....

Blood

Possible Meanings: Flow, pain, passion (life's blood), compassion, circulation.

Points to Consider: Are you bleeding? Are you watching someone else bleed? Is your life being drained, or are you sharing and giving life?

Your Interpretation:

....

....

....

....

Boat

Possible Meanings: Buoyancy, being on top, compatibility (in the same boat), escape, going under.

Points to Consider: Are you in the boat or trying to get into the boat? Who is in the boat with you? What emotions are you trying to transcend?

Your Interpretation:

....

....

....

....

Body Parts

Also see "The Body," page xiii, for a general overview.

Possible Meanings: Hands—grasping/feeling; Feet—mobility/grounding; **Head**—thinking/controlling; **Neck**—support/pain; **Genitals**—fertility/creation/power (also see "Genitals," page 55).

Teeth—first, consider whether you may need to visit the dentist. Your body may be telling you that there's something wrong. If your teeth are loose, it may signify feeling strong enough to salvage a problem at hand, or, if you dream you are young and losing teeth, your consciousness is being elevated. Further, if you dream of a child losing teeth or that you are a child losing teeth, it may signify unexpected abundance (the tooth fairy). If you are getting on in years and dream of loose teeth, it may mean loss of self-image, youth, and self-reliance. If you are younger, it may mean careless speech; and if middle-aged, it could mean falsehoods and foul language.

If your teeth are falling out, you may believe that it is too late to solve a problem at hand. Some Mediterranean cultures believe that if you have this dream, it signifies death at some level—not literal death, but great change. It may also mean loss of masculinity if you are male, or loss of the masculine aspect if you are female. Finally, consider your ethnic background. Teeth falling out may have something to do with loss of face or being embarrassed by your peers.

Points to Consider: Is the body part free and mobile? Is it stiff or in pain? Is it yours or someone else's?

Your Interpretation:

Bones

Possible Meanings: Support, structure, connection, hidden meanings (skeletons in the closet), revelations.

Points to Consider: Are the bones covered or exposed? Are you feeling brittle? Is there something you're trying to hide?

Your Interpretation:

Book

Possible Meanings: Record of events, judgment (judging a book by its cover), knowledge, communication, being authoritative.

Points to Consider: Are you reading or writing a book? Are you judging someone, or is someone judging you? Do you need to read between the lines?

Your Interpretation:

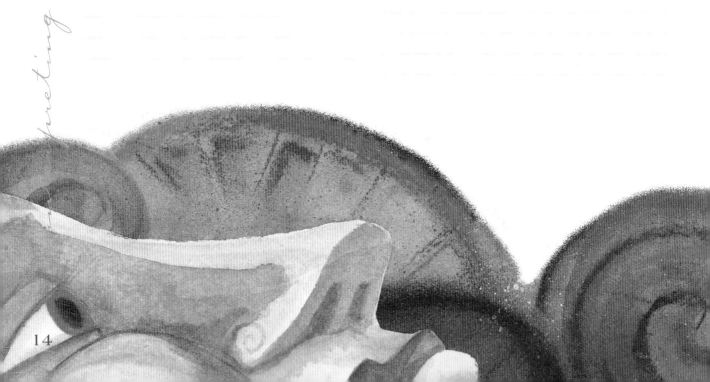

Bookcase

Possible Meanings: Knowledge, order, selection, shelving or storing ideas.

Points to Consider: What kind of books are on the bookcase? Are they your books or someone else's? Are you putting off for tomorrow what you could be doing today (shelving your responsibilities)?

Your Interpretation:

Boots

Possible Meanings: Protection, travel, work, polish, a recap.

Points to Consider: Are the boots comfortable? Are they practical? Do you need protection?

Your Interpretation:

Bottle

Possible Meanings: Message, refreshment, transparency, becoming narrow (bottleneck), intoxication (hit the bottle).

Points to Consider: Is there a message in the bottle? Do you feel bottled up? Is there refreshment to be enjoyed?

Your Interpretation:

Box

Possible Meanings: Containment, gifts, danger (Pandora's box), surprise, practicality.

Points to Consider: Are you in the box? Are you giving or receiving the box? What are you trying to keep contained in your life?

Your Interpretation:

....

....

....

Bread

Possible Meanings: Money, abundance, life, sustenance, livelihood.

Points to Consider: Are you baking the bread or eating it? Have you enough of it? Do you want more?

Your Interpretation:

....

....

....

Bracelet

Possible Meanings: Gift, ownership, ornament, control (handcuffs), identification.

Points to Consider: Are you wearing the bracelet for identification? Is the bracelet restricting you? Who gave you the bracelet?

Your Interpretation:

....

....

....

....

Bridge

Possible Meanings: Link, pathway, transition, safety, extension.

Points to Consider: Are you building a bridge over troubled waters? Are you trying to connect different thoughts? Are you on the bridge or looking at it?

Your Interpretation:

....

....

....

....

Broom

Possible Meanings: Cleaning, romance (swept off your feet), removal, avoidance (sweeping it under the carpet), exaggeration (a sweeping statement).

Points to Consider: Are you being swept off your feet? Are you sweeping something under the carpet? Does something need cleaning up?

Your Interpretation:

Brother

See "Family," page 50.

Bugs

See "Insects," page 63.

Ball

See "Animals," page xiii.

Burglar

Possible Meanings: Intrusion, loss, invasion, sneakiness, dishonesty.

Points to Consider: Are you breaking into something, or are you being broken into? What is being/has been stolen? What are you stealing?

Your Interpretation:

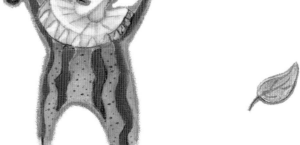

Bus

Possible Meanings: Fixed route, carrier, broken journey, communal thoughts/ideas, passenger.

Points to Consider: Are you part of a group that is heading in the same direction? Do you want to get off the bus, or are you climbing aboard? Do you feel like a passenger rather than a leader?

Your Interpretation:

Butter

Possible Meanings: Change, stress, rancidness, complementarity, companionship (bread and butter), compatibility.

Points to Consider: Are you being spread too thin? Do you want to transform/change an area of your life? Are you looking for companionship?

Your Interpretation:

Butterfly

Possible Meanings: Transformation, beauty, lightness, something shortlived, joy.

Points to Consider: What's visibly changing in your life? Do you want to be noticed? Life is short: Is it time to live it up?

Your Interpretation:

Cab

Possible Meanings: Transportation, arrangements, movement, being escorted, employment.

Points to Consider: Are you driving the cab? Are you sitting in the back (taking a back seat)? Are you giving directions?

Your Interpretation:

Cabin

Possible Meanings: Retreat, nature, privacy, vacation, relaxation.

Points to Consider: Are you in the cabin? Is someone in there with you? Is the cabin in nature or on a ship?

Your Interpretation:

Cage

Possible Meanings: Protection, control, limitations, imprisonment, ownership.

Points to Consider: Who is in the cage? Do you feel protected or imprisoned? How wide is the space between the bars—that is, can you get out easily or are you trapped?

Your Interpretation:

Cake

Possible Meanings: Celebration, joy; apprehension (that is, a birthday cake and the prospect of getting older); guilt, sweetness.

Points to Consider: Is it your cake? Did you bake it? Does everything seem to be going your way at the moment (having your cake and eating it, too)?

Your Interpretation:

Calendar

Possible Meanings: A passage of time, important reminders, a record of time, appointments, organization.

Points to Consider: Are you looking forward to something? Did you forget something/someone? Is there an important appointment coming up?

Your Interpretation:

Candle

Possible Meanings: Dedication, light, blessings, illumination, romance.

Points to Consider: Is the candle shedding light on you? Is it burning strong, or can it be easily blown out? Who lit the candles?

Your Interpretation:

Candy

Possible Meanings: Sweetener, decay (teeth), reward, lust, bribery.

Points to Consider: Are you giving the candy to someone? Is someone giving the candy to you? Are you eating the candy?

Your Interpretation:

Cane (walking stick)

Possible Meanings: Support, protection, mobility, prestige, power.

Points to Consider: Is the cane helping you get about? Are you using the cane for protection? Does the cane make you feel powerful?

Your Interpretation:

23

Car

Also see "Journeys," page xv.

Possible Meanings: You (that is, you are the car), transportation, debt, mobility, awareness.

Points to Consider: Is the car a representation of you? Who is in the driver's seat? How aware are you of your surroundings?

Your Interpretation:

....

....

....

....

Cards

Possible Meanings: Luck, skill, prophecy, shuffling, dealing (that is, being dealt with).

Points to Consider: Who is dealing the cards? Do you feel something is being dealt with? Are you feeling lucky?

Your Interpretation:

....

....

....

....

Carpet

Possible Meanings: Worth; hidden danger (that is, dust, dust mites); affluence; comfort; denial (sweeping it under the carpet).

Points to Consider: Are you walking on the carpet? Are you allergic to the carpet? Is there anything you're hiding?

Your Interpretation:

....

....

....

....

Cat

Possible Meanings: Resilience (nine lives), companionship, independence, stealth, domestication.

Points to Consider: Is the cat wild or domesticated? Are you feeling strong and resilient? Do you feel you are being hunted, or are you doing the hunting?

Your Interpretation:

Cave

Possible Meanings: Sanctuary, hibernation, the subconscious, darkness, adventure.

Points to Consider: Does the cave make you feel claustrophobic or enthused? Is there someone in the cave with you? Do you want them to be there?

Your Interpretation:

Cemetery

Possible Meanings: Completion, dead end, rest, peace, burial.

Points to Consider: Are you walking through the cemetery or running? What is your purpose for being there? Are you frightened or at peace with yourself?

Your Interpretation:

Chains

Possible Meanings: Control, weight, immobility, links, restraint.

Points to Consider: Are the chains on you or someone else? Can they be easily broken? Can you walk around with the chains on?

Your Interpretation:

Chalk

Possible Meanings: Explanations, tuition, something easily removed, diversity, transition.

Points to Consider: Are you using the chalk or watching someone else use it? Are you comparing yourself to someone completely different from you? What do you need to learn?

Your Interpretation:

Chair

Possible Meanings: Support, groundedness, being official, work, meetings.

Points to Consider: Are you sitting on the chair? Is it strong enough to support you? Are you giving the chair to someone else?

Your Interpretation:

26

Chess

Possible Meanings: Strategy, forward thinking, planning, competition, power.

Points to Consider: Are you playing chess or observing? Are you winning or losing the game? Is one of the pieces more significant than the others?

Your Interpretation:

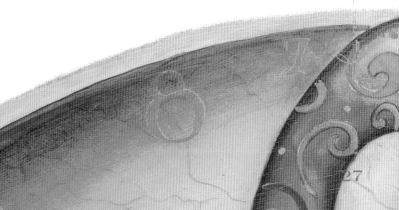

Children

Possible Meanings: Possibilities, commitments, potential, joy, the past.

Points to Consider: Are you the child? Are you playing with children? Do the children bring you joy or heartache?

Your Interpretation:

Chicken

Possible Meanings: Sustenance, cowardice, riddles (what came first—the chicken or the egg), pecking order, hard work.

Points to Consider: Are you the chicken? Is something holding you back (that is, are you unable to fly)? Is the chicken alive or cooked?

Your Interpretation:

Chimney

Possible Meanings: Release, passage, ventilation, escape, waste.

Points to Consider: Is there something/some-one going up in smoke? Is it time to elevate some of your ideas? Do you want to release something/someone from your life?

Your Interpretation:

Chocolate

Possible Meanings: Pleasure, luxury, gratification, sensuality, surprises.

Points to Consider: Are the chocolates a gift, or are you giving the chocolates? Are they hard or soft centers? Do the chocolates make you feel guilty, or are you enjoying them?

Your Interpretation:

Christmas Tree

Possible Meanings: Joy, companionship, family, decorations, gifts.

Points to Consider: Is the tree decorated or bare? Is it in the house or outside? Are there gifts underneath the tree?

Your Interpretation:

Church

See "Places of Worship," page xv.

Climbing

Possible Meanings: Ascension, skill, strength, conquest, higher ground.

Points to Consider: Are you climbing to achieve greater things or to get away? How dangerous is your climb? Are you climbing up or down?

Your Interpretation:

Clock (includes any timepiece)

Possible Meanings: Custodian of time, focus, appointments, indicator, synchronization.

Points to Consider: Are you working around the clock? Do you feel that time is running out, or do you have plenty of time? Are you organized, or do you need to become more organized?

Your Interpretation:

Closet

Possible Meanings: Storage, hidden danger (skeletons in the closet), revelations (coming out of the closet), hideaway, reflection.

Points to Consider: Is there something hidden in the closet? Is there something in the closet that needs airing? Are you unhappy with the persona (mask) you are reflecting to the world?

Your Interpretation:

Clothes

Possible Meanings: Warmth, protection, prominence, role playing, appearance.

Points to Consider: Do you feel as though you're being judged by appearances? Are you dressing up or dressing down? Do the clothes fit?

Your Interpretation:

Clouds

Possible Meanings: Upliftment, transparency, danger (black clouds), abundance (every cloud has a silver lining), ecstasy (on cloud nine).

Points to Consider: Are you looking up at the clouds or flying through the clouds? Are they dark and menacing, or white and welcoming? Does the sun shine through the clouds?

Your Interpretation:

Clown

Possible Meanings: Something make-believe, joy, hidden emotion, laughter, foolishness.

Points to Consider: Are you the clown? Do you feel like a fool in front of others, or are you making people happy? Are you hiding something (that is, what is lurking underneath the makeup)?

Your Interpretation:

Coat

Possible Meanings: Protection, warmth, external layers, dignity, exposure.

Points to Consider: Are you wearing the coat? Is the coat keeping you warm? Is the coat new or in tatters?

Your Interpretation:

....

....

....

Coffee

Possible Meanings: Dependence, rejuvenation, alertness, respite, energy.

Points to Consider: Is the coffee hot and palatable or lukewarm and tasteless? Does the coffee relax you or make you hyperactive? Are you dependent on the coffee?

Your Interpretation:

....

....

....

....

Coins

Also see "Money," pages xv and 82.

Possible Meanings: Luck, prosperity, rewards, wealth, acknowledgment.

Points to Consider: Are the coins easy to carry or a burden? What are you using the coins for? Are you afraid of losing the coins, or do you feel confident and rewarded?

Your Interpretation:

....

....

....

....

Computer

Possible Meanings:
Organization, efficiency, logic, being progressive or informed.

Points to Consider: What information are you storing? Is there information you are trying to retrieve? Are you organized and efficient, or would you like to be?

Your Interpretation:

Corn

Possible Meanings: Abundance, growth, something out of date (corny), inner wealth, a staple.

Points to Consider: Are they corn kernels, or is the corn in the field? Do you feel corny and outdated? Does someone else appear corny and outdated to you?

Your Interpretation:

Cow

See "Animals," page xiii.

Crab

Possible Meanings: Armor, protection, soft interior, annoyance (crabbiness), sideways moving.

Points to Consider: Are you moving sideways instead of forward? Who in your life has a tough exterior but a warm heart? What are you arming yourself against?

Your Interpretation:

Cross

Possible Meanings: Righteousness, purity, sacrifice, dedication, religion.

Points to Consider: Are you looking for salvation? Do you feel that someone is crucifying you? Are you making too many sacrifices?

Your Interpretation:

....

....

....

....

Crow

Possible Meanings: Hoarding, scavenging, darkness, showing off, easily fooled (scarecrow).

Points to Consider: Is the crow easily scared off or powerfully standing its ground? Is it time to get rid of something/someone in your life? Do you feel that someone is taking you for granted, or are you taking someone else for granted?

Your Interpretation:

....

....

....

33

Crowd

Possible Meanings: Anonymity (being lost in the crowd), group effort, pushiness, being stifled, closeness.

Points to Consider: Are you a part of the crowd or observing? Do you feel you are being crowded by people? What crowd are you a part of?

Your Interpretation:

Crown

Possible Meanings: Power, acknowledgment, value, respect, dignity.

Points to Consider: Are you wearing the crown, or do you want to wear it? Is it light or heavy to wear? Do you place the crown on your head, does someone else place it on your head, or do you place it on someone else's head?

Your Interpretation:

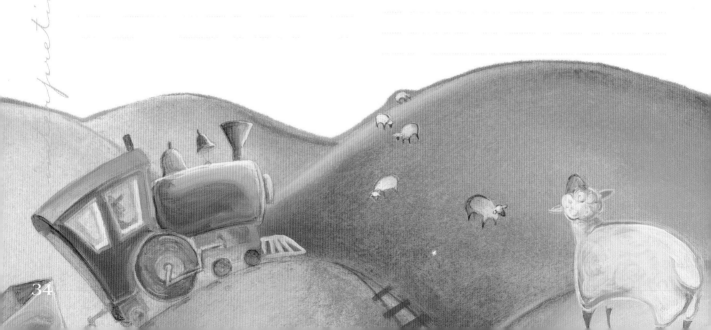

Crying

Possible Meanings: Emotional release, joy, bringing something to attention or to the surface, vulnerability.

Points to Consider: Who is crying? Are they tears of joy or sorrow? Do you want to release something from your life?

Your Interpretation:

....

....

....

Crystal

Possible Meanings: Mystical power, something unearthed, transmitter, dedication, energy.

Points to Consider: Are you receiving or giving the crystal? Are you clear on what you want? Is there something you want to amplify in your life?

Your Interpretation:

....

....

....

Cup

Possible Meanings: Containment, function, an offering, prize, covering.

Points to Consider: Is the cup half full or half empty? Is someone honoring you (that is, are you receiving a cup)? Are you being offered something?

Your Interpretation:

....

....

....

Curtains

Possible Meanings: Completion (final curtain), privacy, exclusion, embellishment, protection.

Points to Consider: Are the curtains open or closed? Do the curtains keep you in the dark? Are they too ornate for the room or their surroundings (that is, out of place)?

Your Interpretation:

....

....

....

Cushion

Possible Meanings: Comfort, support, soft, rest, guarding (cushioning a blow).

Points to Consider: Do you feel you are light and fluffy, or are others treating you this way? Do you need more rest in your life? Are you looking for support?

Your Interpretation:

....

....

....

....

D
to
E

Daughter

See "Family," page 50.

Death

Also see "Death," page xiii.

Possible Meanings: Completion, new beginnings, transformation, change, departure.

Points to Consider: Are you ready for change? Is there someone else whom you wish would change? Is there a part of you that is dying?

Your Interpretation:

Dentist

Possible Meanings: Pain, aggravation, extraction, relief, beautification.

Points to Consider: Is there something that needs to be removed from your life? Is something aggravating you? Does something need straightening out?

Your Interpretation:

Desert

Possible Meanings: Desolation, barrenness, extreme conditions, isolation, dehydration.

Points to Consider: Are you in the desert? How did you end up in the desert? Are things taking a while to grow in your life?

Your Interpretation:

Desk

Possible Meanings: Work, commitment, study, authority, order.

Points to Consider: Are you sitting behind or in front of a desk? Do you feel empowered or snowed under? Is it time to make commitments in your life?

Your Interpretation:

Diamonds

Possible Meanings: Strength, power, affluence, abundance, desirability.

Points to Consider: Are you wearing the diamonds, or do you keep them locked up? Do you feel powerful with them on, or are you scared you may lose them? Are the diamonds clean and polished, or uncut?

Your Interpretation:

Dictionary

Possible Meanings: Definitions, explanations, clarity, discovery, help.

Points to Consider: Are you reading the dictionary? Are you trying to define yourself in some way? Are you looking for an explanation, or would you like to explain yourself?

Your Interpretation:

Divorce

Possible Meanings: Separation, completion, new directions, dissolution, disputes.

Points to Consider: Is there someone/something you want to separate from? What needs to be dissolved? Are you trying to split something up?

Your Interpretation:

Doctor

Possible Meanings: Health, warning, diagnosis, prescription, authority.

Points to Consider: What needs healing? What beliefs do you subscribe to? Are you in a position of authority, or does someone else have authority over you?

Your Interpretation:

Dog

Also see "Animals," page xiii.

Possible Meanings: Friendship, loyalty, love, protection, guidance.

Points to Consider: Who owns the dog? Is the dog offering protection? Do you feel safe with the dog, or are you frightened?

Your Interpretation:

Dolphin

Possible Meanings: Communication, intelligence, playfulness, guidance, uniqueness.

Points to Consider: Do you wish to be seen as unique? Are you looking for guidance? Is it time to loosen up and play?

Your Interpretation:

Donkey

See "Animals," page xiii.

Door

Possible Meanings: New opportunities, access, entry, threshold, success.

Points to Consider: Are doors opening up for you? Is someone slamming a door in your face? Are you closing a door on someone else?

Your Interpretation:

Dove

Possible Meanings: Peace, love, freedom, commitment, message.

Points to Consider: Is someone trying to send you a message? Is it time to make peace with someone/something? Are you hankering for love in your life?

Your Interpretation:

Drinking

Possible Meanings: Replenishment, hydration, sustenance, celebration, survival.

Points to Consider: What are you drinking? Why are you doing so? Did you pour the drink, or was it poured by someone else?

Your Interpretation:

Driving

Possible Meanings: Control, focus, departure, service, manipulation.

Points to Consider: Who is in the driver's seat? Are you in control or trying to regain control? Is someone driving you crazy?

Your Interpretation:

....

....

....

Eagle

Possible Meanings: Power, strength, sovereignty, clear vision, solitude.

Points to Consider: Would you like to soar higher in life? Is it time to spend more time alone? Would you like to achieve higher ideals?

Your Interpretation:

....

....

....

Drum

Possible Meanings: Communication, dance, rhythm, focus, trance.

Points to Consider: Who is beating the drum? To whose beat are you marching? Are you trying to communicate something?

Your Interpretation:

....

....

....

Earrings

Possible Meanings: Ornaments, attention, beautification, value, attraction.

Points to Consider: Do you want to be noticed? Who gave you the earrings? Are they weighing you down?

Your Interpretation:

....

....

....

Ears

See "Body Parts," page 13; and "The Body," page xiii.

Earthquake

Possible Meanings: Disruption, change, scars, wounding, turmoil.

Points to Consider: Is the ground moving underneath you? Do you feel shaken up at the moment? Do you need to give someone else a good shake-up?

Your Interpretation:

Eggs

Possible Meanings: Paradox (the chicken or the egg), wholeness, new potential, sustenance, hidden treasures.

Points to Consider: Do you have an idea waiting to be hatched? Does someone need gentle handling? Are you caught in a paradox?

Your Interpretation:

Elephant

See "Animals," page xiii.

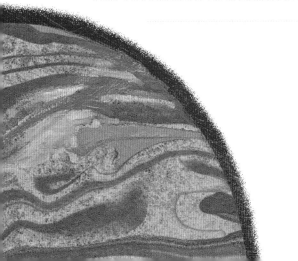

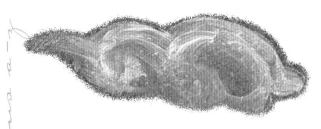

Elevator

Possible Meanings: Movement, ascension, descent, something uplifting, contained.

Points to Consider: Who is riding the elevator? Are you going up or coming down? Are you stuck in the elevator?

Your Interpretation:

Envelope

Possible Meanings: Message, announcement, communication, surprise, invitation.

Points to Consider: Is the envelope addressed to you or someone else? Is there something you want to communicate/announce? Is an important event coming up?

Your Interpretation:

Eyes

See "Body Parts," page 13; and "The Body," page xiii.

46

F
to
G

Face

See "Body Parts," page 13; and "The Body," page xiii.

Your Interpretation:

Fairy

Possible Meanings: Magic, blessings, joy, desires, nature.

Points to Consider: Are you the fairy? Would you like to move closer to nature? Do you have unfulfilled desires?

Your Interpretation:

Falling

Possible Meanings: Out of control, being ungrounded or unsupported, in a slump, descent.

Points to Consider: Do you feel frightened? Does your life feel out of control? Do you see yourself landing?

Your Interpretation:

Fame

See "Star," page 110.

Family

Possible Meanings: Inclusion, identification, familiarity, heritage, kinship.

Points to Consider: Which family member are you with? What is your personal relationship to this individual? Is this person *you* in disguise? Do you feel loved or detached?

Your Interpretation:

Father

See "Family," above.

Feet

See "Body Parts," page 13; and "The Body," page xiii.

Fence

Possible Meanings: Containment, safety, demarcation, defense, barrier.

Points to Consider: Are you fenced in? Are the fences easy to climb over? Are you trapped behind the fence, or do you have someone else trapped?

Your Interpretation:

Fire

Possible Meanings: Purification, cleansing, passion, creation, warmth.

Points to Consider: What are your burning desires? Are you trying to heat something up? Are you running from fire?

Your Interpretation:

Fish

Possible Meanings: Spirituality, weightlessness, abundance, flow, resilience.

Points to Consider: Is the fish representative of you? Are you eating the fish? Are you trying to catch a fish?

Your Interpretation:

....

....

....

Flag

Possible Meanings: Respect, dedication, allegiance, tribute, honor.

Points to Consider: Are you saluting a flag? Do you feel honored in some way? Is someone commanding respect, perhaps you?

Your Interpretation:

....

....

....

Flood

Possible Meanings: Powerful emotion, all-consuming feelings, unexpectedness, feeling that it's time to move, being overwhelmed.

Points to Consider: Are you flooded with emotion? Is the tide of life sweeping you away? Would you like to elevate your thoughts to higher ground?

Your Interpretation:

....

....

....

Flower

Possible Meanings: Blooming, attraction, sensuality, upliftment, acknowledgment.

Points to Consider: Are you giving or receiving flowers? Do you think that life is blooming for you? What is unfolding for you at the moment?

Your Interpretation:

....

....

....

51

Flute

See "Musical Instruments," page 84.

Flying

Possible Meanings: Freedom, inspiration, elevation, overview, detachment.

Points to Consider: Are you flying or watching someone else fly? Is it effortless or challenging? What do you see above or beneath you?

Your Interpretation:

....

....

....

....

Fog

Possible Meanings: Lack of clarity, mystery, dampness, vagueness, confusion.

Points to Consider: Is the fog surrounding you? Is the fog around others? Does the fog clear?

Your Interpretation:

....

....

....

....

Foreign Country

Also see "Geographical Locations," page xiv; and "Journeys," page xv.

Possible Meanings: Adventure, new horizons, concerns, greater understanding, backtracking.

Points to Consider: Do you feel like you're reliving a past-life in the dream? How do you feel about the place you're in? What new adventures are to be undertaken?

Your Interpretation:

....

....

....

Fountain

Possible Meanings: Refreshment, pleasure, beautification, recycling, display.

Points to Consider: Are you trying to get people's attention? Are you drinking from the fountain? Is the fountain a source of relief?

Your Interpretation:

Frog

Possible Meanings: Major transformation, adaptability, major leaps, not being heard (frog in the throat), faith.

Points to Consider: Are you taking, or would you life to take, a leap of faith? Are you hopping from one idea to another? Are you having trouble communicating an idea or feelings (frog in your throat)?

Your Interpretation:

Friend

See "People," page xv.

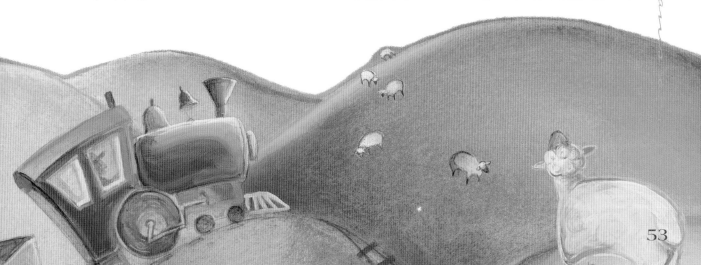

interpreting dreams

Fruit

Possible Meanings: Abundance, bounty, sweetness, reproduction, something forbidden.

Points to Consider: Are you eating the fruit? Is it on a platter? Is the fruit full of seeds (reproduction)?

Your Interpretation:

Garbage

See "Trash," page 118.

Garden

Possible Meanings: Sanctuary, peace, labor, satisfaction, harmony.

Points to Consider: Is it your garden or someone else's? Do you feel at peace? Is it in disarray?

Your Interpretation:

Gate

See "Door," page 43.

Geese

Possible Meanings: Alarm, golden egg, being flustered, equality (what's good for the goose is good for the gander), overreaction.

Points to Consider: Are you being warned about something? Is someone close to you in trouble? Are you searching for equality?

Your Interpretation:

Genitals

Possible Meanings: Fertility, beginnings, ecstasy, dissemination, privacy.

Points to Consider: Whose genitalia is it? Is it male or female? Does it embarrass or excite you?

Your Interpretation:

Gloves

Possible Meanings: Protection, covering, elegance, warmth, being caught (pitcher's glove).

Points to Consider: What is the purpose of the gloves? Are you wearing them for protection, or is someone else wearing them to protect themselves from you? Do you feel you have a good grip on life?

Your Interpretation:

Goat

See "Animals," page xiii.

Gold

Possible Meanings: Power, abundance, danger, respect, envy.

Points to Consider: Is the gold weighing you down? Does the gold make you feel more powerful? Are you trying to hide the gold?

Your Interpretation:

Graduation

Possible Meanings: Acknowledgment, success, completion, elevation, qualifications.

Points to Consider: Are you graduating? Is there somebody with you? Do you feel happy or sad?

Your Interpretation:

....

....

....

Grapes

Possible Meanings: Sensuality, being spoiled, intoxication, envy (sour grapes), communication (grapevine).

Points to Consider: Are you listening to too much gossip? Are you envious of someone, or is someone envious of you? Are you being spoiled, or are you spoiling someone else?

Your Interpretation:

....

....

....

Granddaughter, Grandfather, Grandmother, Grandson

See "Family," page 50.

Grave

Possible Meanings: Ending, submersion, completion, danger (graveyard shift), seriousness.

Points to Consider: Whose grave is it? Are you trying to bury something? Is more time needed for contemplation?

Your Interpretation:

....

....

....

Guitar

See "Musical Instruments," page 84.

Hair

Possible Meanings: Growth, extension, desirability, vitality, announcements, identity.

Points to Consider: Is your hair falling out in the dream? What color is the hair? Do you need to pay more attention to your thoughts?

Your Interpretation:

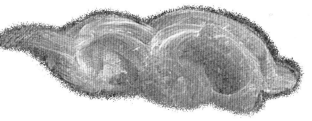

Hammer

Possible Meanings: Strength, power, submission, harm, bullying.

Points to Consider: Is someone trying to bully you? Are you in danger? Is it time to show your power?

Your Interpretation:

Handkerchief

Possible Meanings: Separation, departure, illness, removal, gift.

Points to Consider: Is someone leaving you: a girlfriend, family member, work colleague—or are you leaving them? Are you ill? Is someone giving you a handkerchief, or are you giving someone else a handkerchief?

Your Interpretation:

Hands

See "Body Parts," page 13; and "The Body," page xiii.

Harp

See "Musical Instruments," page 84.

Hat

Possible Meanings: Protection, practicality, elevation, respect, prominence.

Points to Consider: Whose head is the hat on? Is it covering something, or is it a mark of approval? Are you covering your thoughts?

Your Interpretation:

Heaven

Possible Meanings: Rewards, peace, high aspirations, completion, bliss.

Points to Consider: Who is in heaven? Do you feel rewarded or disappointed? Who is with you?

Your Interpretation:

Hell

Possible Meanings: Illusion, punishment, retribution, anger, fear.

Points to Consider: Who is in hell? Are you scared, or do you feel comfortable? Are you going to hell or trying to escape from it?

Your Interpretation:

....

....

....

....

Helmet

See "Hat," page 60.

Horse

See "Animals," page xiii; and "Saddle," page 103.

Hospital

Possible Meanings: Recuperation, life support, ignorance, dedication, attention.

Points to Consider: Who is in the hospital? What signs are you ignoring? Does someone close to you need attention?

Your Interpretation:

....

....

....

....

Hotel

Possible Meanings: Rest, pampering, hospitality, romance, business.

Points to Consider: Why are you in a hotel? Are you enjoying a romantic getaway, or are you on a business trip? Are you playing lip service to someone, or is someone playing lip service to you?

Your Interpretation:

....

....

....

....

House

See "Home," page xiv.

Husband

See "Family," page 50.

Ice

Possible Meanings: Transformation, distance, cooling off, redefining or solidifying something.

Points to Consider: What emotions need to be looked at in the cold light of day? Is someone giving you, or are you giving someone, the cold shoulder? Is there a need for you to get tough?

Your Interpretation:

....

....

....

....

Ice Cream

Possible Meanings: Treat, softness, sweetness, variety, being chilled (that is, chilled out).

Points to Consider: Who gave you the ice cream? Are you eating the ice cream? Is something/someone calling for you to be soft and sweet?

Your Interpretation:

....

....

....

....

Infant

See "Baby," page 6; and "Children," page 27.

Ink

Possible Meanings: Formalities, taking note, clarification, conveyance, protection (an octopus sprays ink when it's in danger).

Points to Consider: Who is using the ink? Are you using the ink to formalize something? Are you looking for protection?

Your Interpretation:

....

....

....

Insects

Possible Meanings: Feeling bugged, peskiness, disdain, diversity, adaptability.

Points to Consider: Is someone bugging you? Do you feel as though you're at the bottom of the food chain? Are you looking for greater diversity in your life?

Your Interpretation:

Invitation

Possible Meanings: Guest, surprise, something that's unexpected, acknowledgment, sociability.

Points to Consider: Who is the invitation from? Are you sending an invitation? Do you feel excluded or included in something?

Your Interpretation:

Island

Possible Meanings: Solitude, retreat, refuge, being surrounded or separated.

Points to Consider: Are you the island? Are you surrounded by emotion (water)? Is it a tropical, carefree island, or is it cold and harsh?

Your Interpretation:

Itch

Possible Meanings: Discomfort, sensation, restlessness, attention, relief.

Points to Consider: What's causing you to scratch? Do you need to be relieved of something/someone? Does someone want to be in partnership with you (that is, you scratch my back, I'll scratch yours)?

Your Interpretation:

Jail

Possible Meanings: Custodian, awaiting something, confinement, apprehension, justice.

Points to Consider: Who is in jail? What side of the bars are you on? Is justice being served, or is a travesty unfolding?

Your Interpretation:

....

....

....

Jar

Possible Meanings: Containment, protection, disharmony (that is, something jars), being unnerved, instability.

Points to Consider: What is in the jar? Is the jar transparent? Is something unnerving to you?

Your Interpretation:

....

....

....

Jewels

Possible Meanings: Reward, power, treasure, bounty, attraction.

Points to Consider: Whose jewels are they? Do they make you feel more desirable, or do you desire them? Are the jewels buried?

Your Interpretation:

....

....

....

Jungle

Possible Meanings: Denseness, diversity, vibrancy, struggle, adventure.

Points to Consider: Can you see the forest through the trees? Are there any clearings? Do you feel threatened, or are you in awe of the jungle?

Your Interpretation:

Kettle

Possible Meanings: Refreshment, announcement, release, being overheated, boredom.

Points to Consider: Are you bored (watching a kettle that never boils)? Are you letting off steam? Do you feel refreshed and rejuvenated?

Your Interpretation:

Key

Possible Meanings: Openings, opportunities, understanding, answers, prominence.

Points to Consider: Is someone handing you the keys? What does the key unlock? Are you looking for answers?

Your Interpretation:

King

Possible Meanings: Elevation, power, respect, subjugation, control.

Points to Consider: Are you the king? Is someone else ruling over you? What is it you want to control?

Your Interpretation:

Kiss

Possible Meanings: Pleasure, intimacy, acceptance, acknowledgment, attraction.

Points to Consider: Are you kissing someone or being kissed? Is it a welcoming kiss, a goodbye kiss, or a passionate kiss? Is something being brought to completion (kissing something goodbye)?

Your Interpretation:

Kitchen

Possible Meanings: Entertainment, sustenance, creativity, sanctuary, service.

Points to Consider: Are you preparing food, or is food being prepared for you? Are you entertaining in the kitchen? Are you out of your depth (that is, you can't stand the heat and it's time to get out of the kitchen)?

Your Interpretation:

Kite

Possible Meanings: Elevation, lofty ideas, freedom, flying high, celebration.

Points to Consider: Who is flying the kite? Is it time to elevate your ideas? Are you celebrating something or enjoying a hobby?

Your Interpretation:

Kitten

See "Cat," page 25.

Knee

See "Body Parts," page 13; and "The Body," page xiii.

Knife

Possible Meanings: Detachment, operation (surgical knife), combat, security, usefulness (Swiss army knife).

Points to Consider: Who is holding the knife? Is it protecting or threatening you? Are you using it for survival?

Your Interpretation:

Ladder

Possible Meanings: Moving up, evolution, promotion, getting ahead.

Points to Consider: Are you going up or down the ladder? Are you making progress? Is the ladder solid or rickety?

Your Interpretation:

Lake

Possible Meanings: Sanctuary, internalizing emotion, vacation, creation (that is, human-made lake), reserve.

Points to Consider: Does the lake represent you? Are you internalizing your emotions? Does the lake represent fun and relaxation, or is it a reserve for future droughts?

Your Interpretation:

Lamb

See "Sheep," page 106.

Lamp

Possible Meanings: Illumination, clarity, vision, understanding, security.

Points to Consider: Is a difficult problem becoming more clear? Do you want to remove unproductive fear from your life? Are you trying to understanding something/someone (that is, shedding light)?

Your Interpretation:

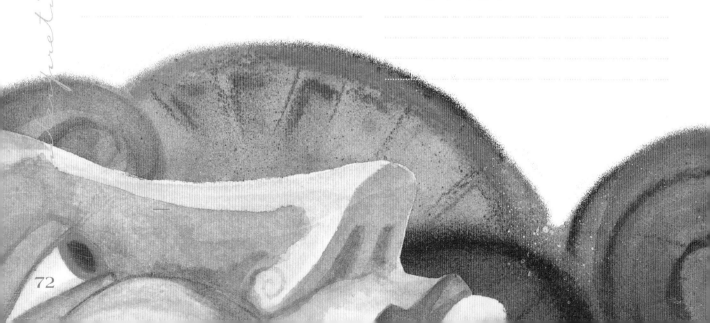

Lawyer

Possible Meanings: Clarification, conflict, justice, knowledge, guidance.

Points to Consider: Are you seeing a lawyer, or is a lawyer cross-examining you? What injustice do you want resolved? Do you or someone else need counseling?

Your Interpretation:

Leaves

Possible Meanings: Detachment, transformation, rebirth, falling, departure.

Points to Consider: Are the leaves falling, have they fallen, or are they still on the tree? Are they green and fresh or brown and brittle? Is there something about yourself you would like to change?

Your Interpretation:

Leeches

Possible Meanings: Release, invasion, extraction, therapy, relief.

Points to Consider: Do you feel as though you are surrounded by parasites? Is something that looks fearful actually supportive? Are your thoughts archaic?

Your Interpretation:

Letter

Possible Meanings: Announcement, information, communication, clarification, news.

Points to Consider: Are you writing a letter, or did you receive one? Does the letter invoke joy or apprehension? What is the message contained in the letter?

Your Interpretation:

Legs

See "Body Parts," page 13; and "The Body," page xiii.

Light

See "Candle," page 22; "Fire," page 50; and "Lamp," page 72.

Lemon

See "Fruit," page 54.

74

Lighthouse

Possible Meanings: Beacon, direction, safety, warning, arrival.

Points to Consider: Does something need greater illumination? Is there something you need to avoid? What warning should you heed?

Your Interpretation:

....

....

....

Lightning

Possible Meanings: Message, clarity, illumination, power, flash.

Points to Consider: Are you receiving an important message? Is it time to change your thinking? Are there storms brewing?

Your Interpretation:

....

....

....

Limousine

Possible Meanings: Extension, exaggeration, affluence, fame, success.

Points to Consider: Are you in the limousine or looking into a limousine? Do you need to bring something to someone's attention? Are you tired of being in control and would prefer to take a back seat?

Your Interpretation:

....

....

....

Lion

See "Animals," page xiii.

Lips

See "Body Parts," page 13; and "The Body," page xiii.

Luggage

Possible Meanings: Vacation, possession, holding on, unresolved issues, a load.

Points to Consider: Do you want to get a load off your mind? Are you carrying around unresolved issues? Is it time for a vacation?

Your Interpretation:

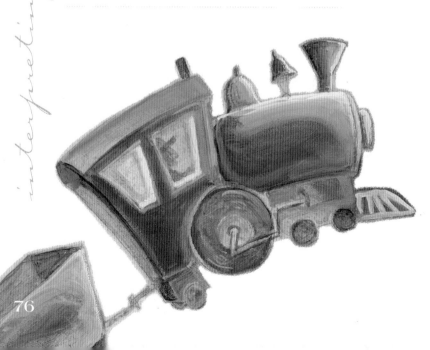

Mail Carrier

Possible Meanings: News, communication, announcements, abundance, commitments.

Points to Consider: Are you the mail carrier? Are you trying to communicate with someone, or is someone trying to communicate with you? Do you feel joyous or anxious?

Your Interpretation:

Mask

Possible Meanings: Camouflage, celebration, being two-faced, hiding, protection.

Points to Consider: Who is wearing the mask? Are you frightened of the mask? Is someone being two-faced?

Your Interpretation:

Marriage

See "Wedding," page 126.

Mattress

Possible Meanings: Comfort, support, pleasure, rest, security.

Points to Consider: Do you need support? Is there someone/something you want to be cushioned from? Do you want to get into bed with someone, or does someone want to get into bed with you?

Your Interpretation:

Meadow

Possible Meanings: Being carefree and natural, liberation, spaciousness, play.

Points to Consider: Are you in the meadow? Are you playing or working? Are there other people with you?

Your Interpretation:

Meat

Possible Meanings: Sustenance, butchery, conquest, domestication, disrespect.

Points to Consider: Are you eating the meat or serving it up? Does the meat repulse you or please you? Are you being treated with disrespect (like a piece of meat)?

Your Interpretation:

Medal

Possible Meanings: Acknowledgment, courage, success, valor, pride.

Points to Consider: Are you wearing the medal? Is someone pinning it on you, or are you giving the medal to someone? Do you think you deserve a medal?

Your Interpretation:

Medicine

Possible Meanings: Relief, healing, punishment, distaste, imbalance.

Points to Consider: Who is taking the medicine? Does it taste sweet or bitter? Do you feel that the medicine is punishing you or healing you?

Your Interpretation:

Mermaid

Possible Meanings: Duality, warning, seduction, temptation, escape.

Points to Consider: Who is the mermaid? Is someone tempting you, or are you seducing someone? Would you like to be able to move in two different worlds?

Your Interpretation:

Milk

Possible Meanings: Kindness, sustenance, growth, love, depletion (has been milked dry).

Points to Consider: Are you drinking the milk? Do you feel strengthened or weakened by the milk? Do you feel someone is milking you for all you're worth?

Your Interpretation:

interpreting dreams a–z

Mirror

Possible Meanings: Reversal, observation, admiration, vanity, truth.

Points to Consider: Are you looking at yourself in the mirror? Do you want to be able to see something more clearly? What image are you projecting?

Your Interpretation:

....

....

....

....

Mist

See "Fog," page 52.

Money

Also see "Money," page xv.

Possible Meanings: Abundance, desire, freedom, energy, power.

Points to Consider: Is money coming in or going out? Is it paper money or coins? Does it make you feel joyful or fearful?

Your Interpretation:

....

....

....

....

Monkey

See "Animals," page xiii.

Moon

Possible Meanings: Femininity, illumination, shadow, rebirth, influence.

Points to Consider: Are you looking up at the moon? Is it shining light on you, or is it creating shadows? Are you pulling someone/something toward you, or is someone/something pulling you toward them/it?

Your Interpretation:

....

....

....

....

Mosquito

See "Insects," page 63.

Moth

See "Insects," page 63.

Mother, Mother-in-Law

See "Family," page 50.

Motorcycle

Possible Meanings: Freedom, adventure, balance, openness, power.

Points to Consider: Who is on the bike? Does the motorcycle give you a feeling of freedom, or are you afraid of falling off? Are you rebelling?

Your Interpretation:

Mountain

Possible Meanings: Knowledge, conquest, elevation, mystery, strength.

Points to Consider: Are you climbing up or down a mountain? Is it an effortless climb or strenuous? Can you see the top?

Your Interpretation:

interpreting dreams a–z

Mouse

See "Animals," page xiii.

Mud

Possible Meanings: Being bogged down, happiness (like a pig in mud), conservative (stick in the mud), slipperiness, play.

Points to Consider: Is something slowing you down? Are you enjoying yourself? Are you bored, or is someone boring you?

Your Interpretation:

Mushroom

Possible Meanings: Food, parasite, hallucination, magic, caution.

Points to Consider: Are you picking the mushrooms or eating them? Are you being warned about someone/something? Do the mushrooms provide sustenance, or are they poisonous?

Your Interpretation:

Musical Instruments

Possible Meanings: Expression, dedication, talent, entertainment, connection.

Points to Consider: Are you playing an instrument, or listening to someone else play one? What does the instrument represent to you? Do you feel uplifted or disappointed?

Your Interpretation:

Nail

Possible Meanings: Completion, attachment, security, capture, piercing.

Points to Consider: Are you hammering a nail? Is a nail being put in or taken out? Are you trying to nail someone/something down?

Your Interpretation:

....

....

....

Nakedness

Possible Meanings: Bareness, being natural and carefree, without defenses, exposure.

Points to Consider: Do you feel uninhibited or exposed? Do you want to reveal the truth about something? Do you feel defenseless?

Your Interpretation:

....

....

....

....

Neck

See "Body Parts," page 13; and "The Body," page xiii.

Nephew

See "Family," page 50.

Nest

Possible Meanings: Home, comfort, marriage, commitment, establishment (building a nest).

Points to Consider: Is there anyone in the nest? Are you making plans for your future (that is, building a nest egg)? Is it time for you to settle down?

Your Interpretation:

....

....

....

....

Net

Possible Meanings: Security, safety, capture, entrapment, collection.

Points to Consider: Is it a safety net, or is someone trying to trap you? Are you trying to catch something? Are you searching for security?

Your Interpretation:

Newspaper

Possible Meanings: Deadlines, advertising, information, relaxation, sensationalism.

Points to Consider: Are you reading the paper, or are you in the paper? Is what you see in the paper pleasurable or painful? Are you focusing on something you should put behind you (that is, yesterday's news)?

Your Interpretation:

Niece

See "Family," page 50.

Nose

See "Body Parts," page 13; and "The Body," page xiii.

Nurse

Possible Meanings: Comfort, support, recovery, dedication, altruism.

Points to Consider: Are you the nurse, or are you being nursed? Do you want to be more dedicated to your career? Are you feeling altruistic?

Your Interpretation:

O to Q

O
to
Q

Oven

Possible Meanings: Creation, preparation, warmth, transformation, diligence.

Points to Consider: Who is cooking? Are your ideas or someone else's half-baked? Is the oven hot or cold?

Your Interpretation:

Owl

Possible Meanings: Knowledge, wisdom, being a predator, healing, omniscience.

Points to Consider: Are you seeking knowledge? Does something need healing in your life? Do you want to see more clearly?

Your Interpretation:

Oar

Possible Meanings: Movement, exercise, leverage, insanity (only one oar in the water), strenuousness.

Points to Consider: Is the oar in or out of the water? Are you rowing with ease or meeting a lot of resistance? Do you need more leverage to get over a challenge?

Your Interpretation:

Ocean

See "Beach," page 9.

Office

Possible Meanings: Work, structure, dedication, responsibility, duty.

Points to Consider: Whose office are you in? Is it a bureaucratic office? Is it tidy or disorderly?

Your Interpretation:

Oil

Possible Meanings: Lubrication, abundance, combustion, mobility, flattery (oil someone up).

Points to Consider: What needs lubrication? Who is being slippery? Are you trying to flatter someone, or is someone trying to flatter you?

Your Interpretation:

Oyster

Possible Meanings: Hidden treasure, lack of feeling, hard exterior, good fortune (world is your oyster), silence.

Points to Consider: Do you feel like an undiscovered treasure? Is someone with a rough exterior being warm and soft toward you? Should you be more silent?

Your Interpretation:

....

....

....

Painting

Possible Meanings: Creativity, expression, value, exhibit, artistry.

Points to Consider: Are you painting or being painted? Are you looking at a painting? Do you feel unappreciated?

Your Interpretation:

....

....

....

Palace

Possible Meanings: Abundance, respect, royalty, aspirations, power.

Points to Consider: Are you looking up at the castle? Do you feel powerful? Are you being unrealistic (that is, building castles in the sky)?

Your Interpretation:

....

....

....

Palm Tree

Possible Meanings: Escape, flexibility, something exotic, relaxation, paradise.

Points to Consider: Are you relaxing under palm trees, or are they in the distance? Do you need to get away? Is it time to be flexible with respect to the needs of others?

Your Interpretation:

....

....

....

Panther

See "Animals," page xiii.

Park

Possible Meanings: Recreation, play, rest, outing, refuge.

Points to Consider: Are you in the park, or can you see a park? Are you watching others play, or are you playing? Is the park surrounded by a concrete jungle?

Your Interpretation:

Pearls

Possible Meanings: Value, delicacy, transformation, irritation, manifestation.

Points to Consider: Do you feel undiscovered (that is, a hidden treasure)? Are you trying to attract someone's attention, or is someone trying to catch your attention? Has something painful in your life actually been a blessing?

Your Interpretation:

Pen or Pencil

Possible Meanings: Communication, authority, message, enclosure, confirmation.

Points to Consider: Are you writing, or is someone else writing? What color is the ink or the lead? Are you being creative, or are you using the pen or pencil to sign something official? Does something need to be aired?

Your Interpretation:

Penis

See "Genitals," page 55.

Perfume

Possible Meanings: Seduction, pleasure, enhancement, attraction, identity.

Points to Consider: What impression do you want to give? Are you or is someone else covering something up? Does someone want to attract your attention, or do you want to attract someone else's attention?

Your Interpretation:

Photograph

Possible Meanings: Memories, frozen moments, nostalgia, records, proof.

Points to Consider: Who is in the photograph? How do you feel about the photograph? Are you feeling nostalgic about something/someone?

Your Interpretation:

Piano

See "Musical Instruments," page 84.

Picnic

Possible Meanings: Outing, friendship, nature, excursion, feeling carefree.

Points to Consider: Have you been invited on a picnic? Do you need to see more of your family and friends? Do you wish things were more simple?

Your Interpretation:

Poison

Possible Meanings: Danger, destruction, impairment, toxins, venom.

Points to Consider: Are you giving the poison to someone, or is someone giving it to you? What dangers are being camouflaged in your life? Is someone poisoning your mind with lies?

Your Interpretation:

Pig

See "Animals," page xiii.

Pillow

See "Cushion," page 36.

Potatoes

See "Food," page xiv.

Pregnancy

Possible Meanings: New beginnings, transportation, expansion, pain, fertility.

Points to Consider: Who is pregnant? Do you want to give birth to new ideas? Is something in your life gestating?

Your Interpretation:

Priest

Possible Meanings: Authority, mediation, dedication, being an intermediary, knowledge.

Points to Consider: Who is the priest? Is someone in your life doing one thing and saying another? Are you looking for a go-between?

Your Interpretation:

Prison

See "Jail," page 65.

Pyramid

Possible Meanings: Mystery, secrets, energy, history, monuments.

Points to Consider: What mysteries do you want to unfold? What hidden powers do you feel you possess? Do you want to bury something in a grand manner?

Your Interpretation:

Queen

Possible Meanings: Support, sovereignty, power, beauty, privilege.

Points to Consider: Are you ruling over someone, or is someone ruling over you? Are you trying to attract attention? Are you supporting someone in their career?

Your Interpretation:

Quilt

Possible Meanings: Warmth, comfort, kinship, bonding, workmanship.

Points to Consider: Are you on top of or underneath the quilt? Do you wish to bond with someone? Does someone need nurturing?

Your Interpretation:

R to S

R to S

Race

Possible Meanings: Competition, agility, endurance, focus, determination.

Points to Consider: Are you winning the race or being left behind? Who are you competing against? Can you see the finish line?

Your Interpretation:

Rain

Possible Meanings: Relief, release, sustenance, constriction, disappointment.

Points to Consider: Is the rain refreshing and hydrating? Does it make you feel depressed or invigorated? Are you out in the rain or watching it fall from indoors?

Your Interpretation:

Radio

Possible Meanings: Entertainment, information, news, announcements, communication.

Points to Consider: Are you broadcasting, or are you listening to something? Does something in your life need to be finely tuned? Are you listening to the radio for information, or is it a form of entertainment?

Your Interpretation:

Rainbow

Possible Meanings: Good fortune: enlightenment, celebration, peace, transformation.

Points to Consider: Is there change occurring in your life? What breakthroughs have you made? Is there a fortune to be made (that is, the pot of gold at the end of the rainbow)?

Your Interpretation:

Rat

Possible Meanings: Deception, survival, pest, agility, underworld.

Points to Consider: Are you the rat? What is plaguing you? Who is betraying you? Are you betraying someone else?

Your Interpretation:

Rice

See "Food," page xiv.

Ring

Possible Meanings: Commitment, dedication, gift, adornment, cycle.

Points to Consider: Are you wearing the ring? Are you giving someone a ring? Are you entering into a union with someone?

Your Interpretation:

Road

Possible Meanings: Access, movement, connection, pathway, communication.

Points to Consider: Are you on the right path? Is it rocky or smooth? Where is it leading?

Your Interpretation:

River

Possible Meanings: Transformation, flow, sustenance, source, eternity.

Points to Consider: Is the river flowing quickly or slowly? Are you in the river or looking at it? Does the river sustain life, or is it flooding the land?

Your Interpretation:

Rocket

Possible Meanings: Power, projection, new horizons, exploration, universal concepts.

Points to Consider: Who fired the rocket? Are you trying to launch a new idea? Are you in a rocket?

Your Interpretation:

Roof

Possible Meanings: Covering, protection, higher thoughts, summit, elevation.

Points to Consider: Who is on the roof? Are you building a roof? Does something need protection?

Your Interpretation:

....

....

....

....

Rope

Possible Meanings: Binding, security, danger, powerlessness (being tied up), being twisted.

Points to Consider: Are you tied up? Are you using the rope to tie something up? Is someone trying to rope you into something you don't really want to do?

Your Interpretation:

....

....

....

....

Rose

Possible Meanings: Sensuality, love, beauty, awakening (wake up and smell the roses), attraction.

Points to Consider: Is someone giving you the roses, or are you giving the roses to someone? Do you need to watch for hidden thorns? Is someone/something trying to get your attention (that is, wake up and smell the roses)?

Your Interpretation:

....

....

....

....

Running

Possible Meanings: Exercise, escape, endurance, competition, opportunity (in the running).

Points to Consider: What are you running from? Are you running for enjoyment, or do your feel out of breath? Are you in the running for something?

Your Interpretation:

....

....

....

Saddle

Possible Meanings: Comfort, control, subservience, awakenings (back in the saddle), bonding.

Points to Consider: Who is in the saddle? Are you moving harmoniously with the horse, or is the horse out of control? Do you feel you are saddled with burdens, or are you enjoying being back in the saddle?

Your Interpretation:

Salt

Possible Meanings: Life (salt of the earth), preciousness, enhancement, thirst, abundance.

Points to Consider: Is someone passing you the salt, or are you passing it to someone? Is the salt dehydrating you, or do you feel abundant? Who is precious to you, or who are you precious to?

Your Interpretation:

Sailing

See "Boat," page 12; and "Yacht," page 130.

Sand

Possible Meanings: Time, change (shifting sands), instability, play, something loose.

Points to Consider: Are you on are shifting sands? Is this a time of instability in your life? Are you playing in the sand?

Your Interpretation:

School

Possible Meanings: Knowledge, pressure, conformity, regulation, friendship.

Points to Consider: Are you teaching or being taught? Do you like being at school, or do you feel uncomfortable? Are you surrounded by friends, or is it a competitive environment?

Your Interpretation:

Scissors

Possible Meanings: Severance, ceremony, change, danger, creativity.

Points to Consider: Are you or someone else cutting something up? Are you using the scissors to create or destroy? Are you trimming someone's hair, or are the scissors being used for a grand opening?

Your Interpretation:

Sex

Possible Meanings: Creation, desire, passion, bonding, lust.

Points to Consider: Who are you having sex with? Do you want it to end or continue? Do you feel bonded with the person or just lustful?

Your Interpretation:

....

....

....

Shark

Possible Meanings: Predator, scavenger, fear, respect, strength.

Points to Consider: Are you being eaten by a shark, or are you afraid of being eaten by a shark? Is the shark preying on someone/something? Is there a sense of respect for the shark?

Your Interpretation:

....

....

....

Sheep

Possible Meanings: Conformity, simplicity, warmth, caution, pretense.

Points to Consider: Are you conforming to someone/something that makes you feel uncomfortable? Is someone following you blindly? Is someone pretending (that is, a wolf dressed in sheep's clothing)?

Your Interpretation:

....

....

....

....

Shell

Possible Meanings: Communication, home, protection, ornaments, retreat.

Points to Consider: Do you need protection from someone/something? Are you or is someone else hiding from something? Are you using the shell to help you communicate?

Your Interpretation:

....

....

....

Shoes

Possible Meanings: Travel, movement, protection, impression, recreation.

Points to Consider: Are the shoes comfortable? Are you wearing the shoes or using them as a weapon? Are you wearing shoes to make an impression?

Your Interpretation:

Shower

Possible Meanings: Cleansing, baptism, abundance (being showered with gifts), new arrival (baby shower), awakenings.

Points to Consider: Are you in the shower or watching somebody shower? Is it a social occasion? Do you feel rejuvenated?

Your Interpretation:

Shoulder

See "Body Parts," page 13; and "The Body," page xiii.

Silver

Possible Meanings: Anniversary, abundance, malleability, communication, workmanship.

Points to Consider: Is the silver solid or liquid? Are you receiving it, giving it, or crafting it? Is the silver a work of art or something you can use?

Your Interpretation:

Skeleton

Possible Meanings: Support, foundation, secrets (skeletons in the closet), blueprint, copy (skeleton key).

Points to Consider: Have you something to hide? Do you feel that someone is trying to imitate you, or are you trying to imitate someone? Is something being exposed?

Your Interpretation:

Sister

See "Family," page 50.

Sky

Possible Meanings: Freedom, expansion, danger (sky is falling), high ideals (sky's the limit), inspiration.

Points to Consider: Is the sky blue or gray? Do you feel free, or are you about to be rained upon? Are you looking for inspiration?

Your Interpretation:

Snake

Possible Meanings: Transformation, fertility, change, something discarded, cold-blooded.

Points to Consider: Who is being tempted? Does something in your life need a makeover? Is it time to shed something from your life?

Your Interpretation:

Snail

Possible Meanings: Slowness (snail's pace), vulnerability, burdens, something transportable, undesirability.

Points to Consider: Who/what is moving slowly? Do you feel the world is sitting on your shoulders? Are you leaving a trail?

Your Interpretation:

Snow

Possible Meanings: Uniqueness, coldness, purity, play, sport.

Points to Consider: Do you or someone else feel snowed under? Does something/someone need cooling down? Are you playing in the snow or working?

Your Interpretation:

....

....

....

....

Soap

Possible Meanings: Cleansing, drama (soap opera), lathering, sanitizing, punishment (wash mouth out with soap).

Points to Consider: What needs washing? Are you caught up in somebody else's drama or your own? Is someone being vulgar?

Your Interpretation:

....

....

....

....

Son

See "Family," page 50.

Soup

Possible Meanings: Combination, nutrients, warmth, predicament (in the soup), being clouded (pea soup).

Points to Consider: Who is in a predicament? Is the soup nourishing and providing warmth? Is something/someone too hot to handle?

Your Interpretation:

....

....

....

....

interpreting dreams a–z

109

Spider

Possible Meanings: Misunderstanding, crafts-manship, predator, fear, being captured.

Points to Consider: Who is the spider? What tangled web is being woven? Are you over-reacting to something/someone, or is someone overreacting to you?

Your Interpretation:

Stage Fright

Possible Meanings: Exposure, being unprepared or self-conscious; withholding, anticipation.

Points to Consider: Who is in the audience? Are you standing in front of an audience, or are you running away? What barriers stand between you and success?

Your Interpretation:

Stairs

Possible Meanings: Ascension, descent, effort, graduation, elevation.

Points to Consider: Are you going up or down? Can you see the top? Are you struggling to get up the stairs?

Your Interpretation:

Star

Possible Meanings: Beauty, distance, fame, prominence, guidance (guiding star).

Points to Consider: Do you want to be a star, or does someone else? Are you seeking inspi-ration? Are you dazzled by your senses (that is, starstruck)?

Your Interpretation:

Storm

Possible Meanings: Disturbance, commotion, discharge, outburst, crisis.

Points to Consider: Are you caught in a storm or watching a storm? Is there a storm brewing? Is there something you would like to get off your chest?

Your Interpretation:

Sun

Possible Meanings: Illumination, masculinity, radiation, something all-encompassing (everything under the sun), profile.

Points to Consider: Is the sun warming you? Do you want a higher work profile, or does someone else? Are you feeling confident?

Your Interpretation:

Strawberries

See "Fruit" page 54.

Swan

Possible Meanings: Transformation, beauty, misinterpretation, serenity, grace.

Points to Consider: Is someone transforming into a graceful and beautiful being? Are you seeking serenity? Do you feel you are being misinterpreted, or are you misinterpreting someone?

Your Interpretation:

Swimming

Possible Meanings: Exercise, competition, buoyancy, survival (keeping your head above water), adaptability.

Points to Consider: Are you swimming for recreation or trying to get away from something? Are you struggling in the water? Are you adaptable to different people and ideas?

Your Interpretation:

Sword

Possible Meanings: Power, protection, revenge, honor, antagonism (crossing swords).

Points to Consider: Is the sword in your hand or someone else's? Is it sharp or blunt? Is someone annoying you, or are you annoying someone?

Your Interpretation:

T to V

Table

Possible Meanings: Meetings, entertainment, announcements, confession, covertness (under the table).

Points to Consider: Is there something going on under the table? Do you need to announce or air something? Are you socializing or holding a meeting at the table?

Your Interpretation:

Teeth

Also see an extended explanation under "Body Parts," page 13.

Possible Meanings: Youth, power, strength, decay, vanity.

Points to Consider: Are your teeth strong or weak? Are they white or discolored? Are you smiling, or are your teeth clenched?

Your Interpretation:

Tea

Possible Meanings: Refreshment, fortune, prediction, sociability, revolution (Boston Tea Party).

Points to Consider: Are you making the tea, or is someone serving the tea? Is it tea for two? Do you need a rest (tea break)?

Your Interpretation:

Tent

Possible Meanings: Nomad, displacement, something temporary, shelter, outdoors.

Points to Consider: Do you feel nomadic? Are you using the tent for recreational purposes? Is the tent keeping you safe, or is it collapsing?

Your Interpretation:

Test

Possible Meanings: Validation, exposure, judgment, understanding, trial.

Points to Consider: Who is being tested? Are you comfortable or ill at ease? Are you judging someone, or is someone judging you?

Your Interpretation:

Throat

See "Body Parts," page 13; and "The Body," page xiii.

Tidal Wave

Possible Meanings: Attachment, feeling overwhelmed, extreme force, intuition, consciousness.

Points to Consider: What caused the tidal wave? Are you being flooded with emotion? Do you feel overpowered or illuminated?

Your Interpretation:

Time

See "Clock," page 29.

Tongue

See "Body Parts," page 13; and "The Body," page xiii.

Tooth

See "Teeth," page 115.

Torch

Possible Meanings: Illumination, focus, direction, confidence, shining light.

Points to Consider: Who is shining the light? What is the torch shining on? Does something need to be uncovered?

Your Interpretation:

Toys

Possible Meanings: The past, gifts, play, distraction, fantasy.

Points to Consider: Is someone toying with you, or are you toying with someone? Are you dreaming of the past? Are they your toys or someone else's?

Your Interpretation:

Tower

Possible Meanings: Strength, danger, protection, being on guard, imprisonment.

Points to Consider: Who is in the tower? Does the tower make you feel safe, or do you feel confined? Are you feeling strong?

Your Interpretation:

Train

Possible Meanings: Movement, being on track, straightforwardness, punctuality, instruction.

Points to Consider: Are you training someone or being trained? Are you on a rigid path or on the right track? Is someone pulling you along, or do you feel you are pulling too much excess baggage?

Your Interpretation:

....

....

....

Trap

Possible Meanings: Confinement, control, ambush, something being held, silence (shut your trap).

Points to Consider: Is someone talking too much? Is someone trying to trap or ambush you? Is someone trying to control you, or are you trying to control someone else?

Your Interpretation:

....

....

....

Trash

Possible Meanings: Rejection, waste, release, nonsense, worthlessness.

Points to Consider: Are you throwing out the garbage? Do you feel worthless and unloved? What nonsense are you being subjected to?

Your Interpretation:

....

....

....

Treasure

Possible Meanings: Abundance, danger, in hiding, search, something in reserve.

Points to Consider: Who should you be treasuring more? Are you being made aware of hidden talents? Are you waiting for something to be discovered?

Your Interpretation:

....

....

....

Tree

Possible Meanings: Nature, home, sustenance, strength, hidden resources.

Points to Consider: Do you feel firmly grounded, or can you be easily blown over? Are you missing the big picture because you are too focused on one small aspect (that is, can't see the forest through the trees)? What are your hidden resources?

Your Interpretation:

Your Interpretation:

Turkey

See "Food," page xiv; and "Animals," page xiii.

Tunnel

Also see point #5 on page xi.

Possible Meanings: Passage, breakthrough, being one-eyed (tunnel vision), inconspicuousness, subconscious insight.

Points to Consider: Is there light at the end of the tunnel? Do you feel frightened because it is dark and damp, or do you feel relieved because of a new discovery? Who is looking at something with a closed mind?

Umbrella

Possible Meanings: Covering, protection, inclusion, collapse, superstition.

Points to Consider: Who do you want to take under your care, or who wants to take you under their care? Are you worrying about unfounded dangers (that is, an open umbrella in the room)? Are you looking for protection from an emotional downpour?

Your Interpretation:

Uncle

See "Family," page 50.

Unicorn

Possible Meanings: Magic, fantasy, unattainability, abundance, support.

Points to Consider: Are you watching the unicorn or riding it? What is impossible to prove? Are you living in a fantasy, or is abundance on its way?

Your Interpretation:

Vacation

Possible Meanings: Distraction, release, escape, rewards, aspirations.

Points to Consider: Who is on a vacation? Who would you like to send away on a vacation? Is it time for a break, or should you focus on the job at hand?

Your Interpretation:

Vacuum Cleaner

Possible Meanings: Extraction, deception, capture, suffocation, reinforcement.

Points to Consider: Who is using the vacuum cleaner? What hidden dangers need to be removed? Who is living in a vacuum (fantasy world)?

Your Interpretation:

Vagina

See "Genitals," page 55.

Vampire

Possible Meanings: Darkness, myths, parasites, a drain, immortality.

Points to Consider: Who is the vampire? What is about to be stolen, or what do you want to steal? Are you or is someone else afraid of getting old?

Your Interpretation:

Vase

Possible Meanings: Ornament, preciousness, fragility, container, practicality.

Points to Consider: What needs to be shown off? Is the vase cracked? Is it valuable or functional?

Your Interpretation:

Veil

Possible Meanings: Mystery, commitment, ownership, deception, anonymity.

Points to Consider: Who is behind the veil? What cannot be exposed? Are you or is someone else being mysterious?

Your Interpretation:

Vine

Possible Meanings: Extension, intrusion, strength, something stifling, confidence.

Points to Consider: Is someone trying to entangle you? Are you swinging from the vines, or are they strangling you? Does something in your life need expansion?

Your Interpretation:

W to Z

Wall

Possible Meanings: Defense, enclosure, understanding (the writing's on the wall), frustration (being driven up the wall), barrier.

Points to Consider: Is someone driving you up the wall? Does something need to be defended? Are you trying to keep something enclosed?

Your Interpretation:

Wallet

Possible Meanings: Abundance, identification, possession, value, finances.

Points to Consider: Did you find or lose a wallet? Is it full or empty? Are your finances vulnerable?

Your Interpretation:

War

Possible Meanings: Destruction, creation, valor, fear, conflict.

Points to Consider: Who is in conflict? What needs to be destroyed? Are you attacking or defending?

Your Interpretation:

Watch

See "Clock," page 29.

Water

Possible Meanings: Hydration, birth, life, emotion, something cyclical.

Points to Consider: Are you in the water or looking at the water? Are they still waters or violent? What needs recycling?

Your Interpretation:

Waterfall

Possible Meanings: Mystery, descent, prominence, attraction, acceleration.

Points to Consider: Are you looking up or down at the waterfall? Does it have a cave hidden behind it? Does the pressure of the falling water pose a danger?

Your Interpretation:

Waves

See "Beach," page 9; and "Tidal Wave," page 116.

Wedding

Possible Meanings: Announcement, union, bond, celebration, commitment.

Points to Consider: Whose wedding is it? Are you full of apprehension, or is it a celebration? What commitment needs to be announced publicly?

Your Interpretation:

Whale

Possible Meanings: Solitude, impressiveness, good times (whale of a time), being marooned (beached whale), differences.

Points to Consider: Are you having a good time, or do you feel stranded? Do you want to impress someone or be left alone? Who aren't you seeing eye-to-eye with?

Your Interpretation:

....

....

....

Whip

Possible Meanings: Mastery, control, momentum (crack the whip), punishment (whip into shape), ease (whip something up).

Points to Consider: Does something need to be put into motion? Is someone trying to control you, or are you trying to control someone? Are you putting too much effort into something that isn't bringing results?

Your Interpretation:

....

....

....

Wife

See "Family," page 50.

Wig

Possible Meanings: Camouflage, protection, deception, enhancement, mystery.

Points to Consider: Who is wearing the wig? What is being covered up? Would you like your ideas to be more fertile?

Your Interpretation:

....

....

....

Wind

Possible Meanings: Elusiveness, inspiration, discomfort, freedom, intuition.

Points to Consider: Does the wind make you feel uncomfortable, or do you feel free? Is the wind making it difficult to move forward, or is it pushing you forward? Is what you know like the wind—unseen but felt?

Your Interpretation:

....

....

....

....

Window

Possible Meanings: Enlightenment, breakthrough, clarity, escape, opportunity.

Points to Consider: Are you looking out of or into a window? Can you see anything through the window? Is it a window of opportunity?

Your Interpretation:

....

....

....

....

Wine

Possible Meanings: Celebration, blessing, fermentation, intoxication, invigoration.

Points to Consider: What color is the wine? Are you celebrating with the wine or being blessed? Does the wine make you feel rejuvenated or intoxicated?

Your Interpretation:

....

....

....

....

Wings

Possible Meanings: Liberation, movement, flight, being backstage (in the wings), a stance (left or right wing).

Points to Consider: Are you wearing the wings, or is someone else? Is there only one wing? Do you wish you could fly, or are you watching someone else fly?

Your Interpretation:

....

....

....

....

Wolf

Possible Meanings: Masquerade (wolf in sheep's clothing), solitude (lone wolf), teamwork, acknowledgment (wolf whistle), cunningness.

Points to Consider: Are you the hunter, or are you being hunted? Do you need to work as part of a team, or are you a lone wolf? Is someone trying to deceive you?

Your Interpretation:

Work

Possible Meanings: Commitment, expression, definition, reward, livelihood.

Points to Consider: Are you working hard, or is it effortless? Do you feel enslaved or empowered? Is there something you would like to work out?

Your Interpretation:

Worm

Possible Meanings: Being hidden, deviousness (worming out of something), invasion, adaptability, exploration.

Points to Consider: Is someone trying to worm their way into your life? Is the worm digging in or trying to burrow out? What needs to be dug in order to be seen?

Your Interpretation:

X (The Letter)

Possible Meanings: Crossroads, the number 10, signature, multiplication.

Points to Consider: Who drew the *x*? Is it a sign of expansion (multiplication) or mystery (x marks the spot)? Is someone illiterate or uneducated?

Your Interpretation:

Yacht

Possible Meanings: Freedom, extravagance, abundance, recreation, pleasure.

Points to Consider: Are you on a yacht or watching one? Are you in a competition or on the yacht for pleasure? Are you sailing away from land or toward it?

Your Interpretation:

X-ray

Possible Meanings: Vision, exposure, illumination, discovery, examination.

Points to Consider: What needs to be exposed? What discoveries are being made? Does something need further examination?

Your Interpretation:

Zoo

Possible Meanings: Display, confusion, unconventionality, imprisonment, excursion.

Points to Consider: Are you visiting a zoo, or are you in a cage at the zoo? Is it a pleasant outing, or do you feel that the animals should be free? Are things in a state of confusion?

Your Interpretation:

Afterword

I'd like to leave you with a final thought inspired by a story that personal development coach Dr. Wayne Dyer often tells at his seminars. It beautifully expresses the importance of searching for your own truths and answers, and underlies the reason for keeping a personal dream dictionary and dream journal.

Imagine you've woken up in the middle of the night, disorientated and confused. You stumble out of bed and start fumbling for the light switch. You don't find it! Across the street you notice that your neighbors' lights are on. You immediately rush over to look for your light switch on their well-lit walls. Ludicrous, huh? But how often do you run to someone else for advice, opinions, and beliefs when you want illumination in your life? Illumination is with you all the time. It is self-awareness, and it is nurtured when you trust in your own commitments, your own passions, and your own desires. The light switch has always been in your room.

Enjoy your dreams!

About the Author

Leon Nacson (an avid dreamer) was born in Alexandra, Egypt, to Greek parents. He is the founder of *The Planet* newspaper, a well-established publication that covers environmental, health, and personal development issues. Leon facilitates seminars and workshops throughout Australia and Asia for such notable individuals as Louise Hay, Denise Linn, Shakti Gawain, Stuart Wilde, and Deepak Chopra. He can also be heard on Australia's number-one radio station as the resident dream coach. This is Leon's ninth book. He works in Sydney with his sons, Eli and Rhett; and lives with his wife, Colleen, and dog, Astor.

Other Books by Leon Nacson

Aromatherapy for Lovers and Dreamers (co-authored with Judith White and Karen Downes)

Aromatherapy for Meditation and Contemplation (co-authored with Judith White and Karen Downes)

Cards, Stars and Dreams (co-authored with Matthew Favaloro)

Deepak Chopra: World of Infinite Possibilities

Dreamer's Guide to the Galaxy

Dyer Straight

I Must Be Dreaming

Interpreting Dreams A–Z

Simply Wilde (co-authored with Stuart Wilde)

Leon is compiling a new book that will feature dreams from people around the world. If you have an interesting dream you wish to share with others, email: nacson@theplanet.com.au

ACKNOWLEDGMENTS

Rachel and Carol, thank you. Dr. Kal Thomas, thanks for the technical advice. Eris, Jill, Christy, and Jenny, you're the best.

Hay House Lifestyles Titles

Flip Books

101 Ways to Happiness, by Louise L. Hay

101 Ways to Health and Healing, by Louise L. Hay

101 Ways to Romance, by Barbara De Angelis, Ph.D.

101 Ways to Transform Your Life, by Dr. Wayne W. Dyer

Books

A Garden of Thoughts, by Louise L. Hay

Aromatherapy A–Z, by Connie Higley, Alan Higley, and Pat Leatham

Colors & Numbers, by Louise L. Hay

Constant Craving A–Z, by Doreen Virtue, Ph.D.

Dream Journal, by Leon Nacson

Healing with Herbs and Home Remedies A–Z, by Hanna Kroeger

Heal Your Body A–Z, by Louise L. Hay

Home Design with Feng Shui A–Z, by Terah Kathryn Collins

Homeopathy A–Z, by Dana Ullman, M.P.H.

Interpreting Dreams A–Z, by Leon Nacson

Natural Gardening A–Z, by Donald Trotter, Ph.D.

You Can Heal Your Life, by Louise L. Hay

and

Power Thought Cards, by Louise L. Hay

All of the above titles
may be ordered by
calling or faxing Hay House
at the numbers on the
next page.

interpreting dreams a

We hope you enjoyed this Hay House Lifestyles book.
If you would like to receive a free catalog featuring additional
Hay House books and products, or if you would like information
about the Hay Foundation, please contact:

H
LIFE
Styles

Hay House, Inc.
P.O. Box 5100
Carlsbad, CA 92018-5100

(760) 431-7695 or (800) 654-5126
(760) 431-6948 (fax) or (800) 650-5115 (fax)
Please visit the Hay House website at:
www.hayhouse.com